testimonials...

SME's are the cornerstone of the economy yet their survival is plagued by unrelenting competitive constraints and countless challenges. If you're interested in growing your small to medium size enterprise from strength to strength but have come to the realisation that:

· Your innovation practice is stagnating

· There's a disconnect between your value proposition and customer expectations

· Your business model isn't quite as relevant as it once was

· Your marketing data doesn't seem to translate into truly differentiated offerings, or

· The time has come for you to evolve from a product/service based business to a solution based business

... then you need to read this collection of success stories from CEO's who have transformed their companies, by design.

The author, Sam Bucolo is a man driven by a singular vision - that design led SME's will fuel a nation's future prosperity – a vision I wholeheartedly endorse along with this book. To shape the strategy that will ensure your firm's future, immerse yourself in *Are We There Yet?* today.

Enjoy!

Maureen Thurston

Chair, Good Design Australia

In today's rapidly changing world it is essential that firms are able to continuously transform themselves to remain competitive. This is a challenge that cannot be addressed by doing what was done yesterday since yesterday's unique knowledge is today's common practice and hence becomes a table stake rather than a basis for competitive advantage. The one truth that will remain is that being competitive means being simultaneously relevant and cost competitive from the customer's point of view.

In his book *Are We There Yet? insights on how to lead by design* Sam Bucolo provides a practical guide to Design Led Innovation. Design Led Innovation takes its starting point in a deep understanding of the customer's problem and by applying design thinking it enables firms to achieve a high level of relevance from the customer's perspective.

The strength of the book, apart from its practical approach with many case examples, is that it conveys an understanding that to be successful in Design Led Innovation the firm must not only achieve a deep customer understanding, but must also change its managerial mindset and ensure alignment of all its processes and systems to achieve the desired outcome.

I can thoroughly recommend this practical book to firms that desire to embark on the journey of Design Led Innovation.

Göran Roos

Prof. Strategic Management, University of Adelaide

testimonials...

I fully welcome the ideas and suggestions put forward by Sam in this book. As economies such as Australia and the UK face up to new global economic realities, design will play an ever more important role.

As Sam's book highlights, design plays a vital part in innovation, which can improve the competitiveness of large as well as small and medium sized enterprises (SMEs). Design Council's *Leading Business by Design* research documented the impact this approach is having on some of the world's most renowned companies, including Barclays, Diageo, Jaguar Land Rover, Rolls-Royce and Virgin Atlantic.

This is how these companies will stay ahead of their competitors. But as this book shows, a design led approach is increasingly as important for SMEs, who make up 94 per cent of businesses in the UK and 96 per cent in Australia.

Sam's book clearly and successfully outlines the role design can play in driving innovation, helping SMEs to thrive in a rapidly changing world.

John Mathers

CEO, Design Council, UK

BIS Publishers
Building Het Sieraad
Postjesweg 1
1057 DT Amsterdam
The Netherlands
bis@bispublishers.nl
www.bispublishers.nl

All web references were correct at the time of going to press.

ISBN 978 90 6369 409 8
Category: Management / Design / Education / SME

Book Designer: Patrick Forrest
Proof Reader: Chloe de Brito

'are we there yet?

insights on how to *lead by design*

SAM BUCOLO

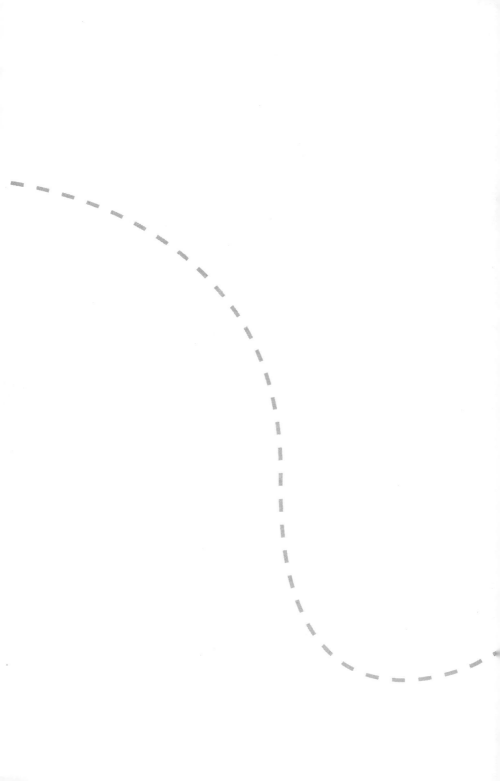

Thanks to my wife Lisa,

and Nathan and Matthew,

for all your love.

Are We There Yet?

contents

Are We There Yet?

foreword

We are emerging from one of the worst economic crises in recent history and every nation needs to build its resilience and competitiveness. Innovation is widely understood as a requirement for our economies to grow, but are our innovation efforts relevant to today's problems? Are we solving the right problems to address the opportunities of today and into the future?

Key to our future prosperity will be the workhorse industry of a nation's economy, the small to medium sized enterprise (SME). Ensuring they remain competitive through innovation will underpin how a nation can maintain its standard of living for future generations. If SMEs are so important to a nation's future, what new models of innovation are they required to adopt to ensure they remain relevant and competitive in rapidly changing economic conditions?

In this book, I will outline that the role of 'design' as an innovation driver squarely addresses this challenge, and that design has a critical role to play in smaller sized industries as well as larger sized firms. Design has been widely explored and well understood at a product or service level. But 'design' can go much further to ensure firms are prepared for the strategic renewal they need to undertake to remain competitive in a new economic construct.

Design Led Innovation (DLI) uses the process and

practices of design, commonly referred to as 'design thinking', as a foundation to apply a set of methods to transform a firm's business model through a deep understanding of its future customers and stakeholders. This ultimately ensures the firm's activities are aligned to creating and capturing value around its core purpose. This is may seem fundamental to good business practice, but the reality is that this is rarely achieved.

It's my hope this book will inspire an interest in the design process as applied to business, in as many people as possible. I hope to encourage the CEO of a SME, for example, to take the first step on the journey to ensuring their company remains relevant in a rapidly changing economic paradigm. Or to help the designer understand what they need to change in their own approach, to ensure their clients remain successful by reframing how design is applied in their company. Throughout the book, I have also shared rich and varied case studies, which demonstrate how students of business and design can change their mindsets and carry this knowledge forward to ensure business they work in will be successful and competitive in the long run.

starting

he conversation

with sam bucolo

starting the conversation
with *sam bucolo*

My name is Sam Bucolo and I have one of the best jobs going. I'm an academic Professor, which fuels my desire to question, build knowledge and stimulate students. But I'm also an academic who has the remit and respect to engage with an industry audience ... I get to challenge them, learn from them, and most importantly, partner with them as they grow and prosper. The unique knowledge I gain while working with these firms helps me inspire future graduates and equip them for the workplace of the future. Ultimately this will make for a stronger and prosperous global society.

I've been encouraged to write this book by colleagues and industry leaders I've worked with, to share the insights I've gained over my career with a wider audience than just my students and the companies I've worked with. However writing is generally not my style, as I prefer to have a conversation – this may be the Italian in me, which enjoys the social nature of learning. I'm most comfortable when I'm in conversation with a group, whether they're students, CEOs, clusters of firms (large or small), or an innovation team within a specific organisation.

At the moment I'm unable to keep up with the number of conversations I'm being asked to have, so I came around to the idea of a book as an efficient way of sharing valuable insights I've gained over many years. Sharing knowledge benefits everyone, and in the case of Design Led Innovation, translates into ensuring firms remain competitive and a future workforce has the skills and knowledge required to support them.

As the book is a conversation, it's been written with this style in mind and therefore I've taken much of the academic speak and theory out of the text. This is not to dumb down the content, but to make it broadly accessible. I understand the time constraints on everyone in today's busy world, and have used the language of business (rather than academia) to make it as practical as possible.

I've tried to make the book a great introduction to Design Led Innovation and include practical stories from a SME perspective. I've purposefully avoided writing the book as another management text of prescriptive descriptions of innovation tools and innovation theory. So I hope the book will be more of a conversation than a "how to innovate" manual.

For those seeking more information on the theory, I've added some key reference and links to documents, which may be of interest. I'm happy to be contacted with questions and if I can't answer them, I'll find someone who can!

Each chapter has been written from common questions that have been directed to me when working with firms through lectures, workshops or mentoring. I draw on the wisdom of CEOs who have challenged me and inspired me. The title of the book reflects the overarching question, which is often asked of me – "So how do we know when we are leading by design?" or, to put it another way, "Are we there yet?"

I hope that the book and the stories I share will prove the significance of this question. The CEOs' stories will illustrate that the journeys they've undertaken to becoming design led were not clear or straightforward and that they wandered off course many times. As with any design project, if we know the answer at the beginning, we're merely solving today's problem. What we need to do is focus on tomorrow's future. The process of design is an experience that must be embraced, which many of the firms I have worked with have realised and profited by. It's through their stories, scattered through this book, that I hope to inspire the start of a journey for many more firms and individuals.

Are We There Yet?

what is *Design Led Innovation?*

This book is not about design, which is the typical question I'm asked when I first start to work with a firm. It's about using the process of design to grow a business.

From an academic perspective, there's been a great deal of research into the importance of design to a firm's success. Most people understand the role of design in the development of new products. But we've come to understand that design can add significant value to a firm's strategic capabilities – going way beyond the development of a product or service. Design is no longer seen as just a downstream-related activity such as adding form or graphics to a product, but is now used to add strategic value to a business.

A successful business goes far beyond a one single element, such as a great product or service. This sounds like a simple proposition, but from my experience most businesses are operating from a narrow perspective that restricts potential to scale their growth. The key to becoming globally competitive in today's economy is a **well-designed business.** This requires adopting a different way of framing situations and possibilities, of doing things, and tackling problems ... essentially a cultural transformation of the way a company undertakes its business.

This union of design and business is referred to as Design Led Innovation (DLI). It's sometimes referred to as design thinking, but as I'll show it's far more than a thinking skill. DLI isn't just an academic term ... it's a practical application that enables businesses to transform themselves to ensure they remain relevant and competitive in uncertain economic conditions.

A good way to understand how design can be applied to an entire business is to think of a product that is well designed, and ask … what makes it well designed? How did the designer achieve the integration of the features, detail, and great form? What was the process? What information did the designer need?

The key is that good design would have started with a deep understanding of the customer's perspective and everything about the design must align with that customer's needs and desires. To get to this point, the designer did not jump to a solution, but explored multiple directions by prototyping ideas with customers. The final result would not be an either - or approach, but it is one of integration around the often contradictory customer insights, which makes the design great.

We've all experienced a product which is not 'exactly right' … a phone with buttons that are too small and the text unreadable; a lamp that is difficult to turn on or adjust; an office chair that seems impossible to adjust to just the right height and tilt. Because we're human we can often adapt to poor product design by adjusting our postures and behaviours, but what happens when a business is poorly designed?

We've all experienced fails when we deal with businesses … test drove a new car that looked great, performed well, but the dealer was so disinterested we spent our money elsewhere; stayed at a hotel with well-appointed rooms and breathtaking views, but poor noise insulation meant a sleepless night; tried to purchase something on the internet only to have the site crash after we've spent 10 minutes feeding in our personal details and credit card number. These are all examples of poorly designed businesses. Sure we can compensate for their poor performance or lack of service, but in an economic environment where product differentiation is critical, ensuring that all aspects of a business have been designed and provide value is critical to growth and success. The irony is that to ensure all parts of a business are integrated is not hard; it just requires a rethink of what the business does and how it delivers on customer value. I'll explain in the coming chapters that this is the first part of leading by design – questioning how innovation is undertaken within a business.

I've found that most businesses have gaps in what they're offering, and this is because they've grown organically from an idea, possibly generations ago. A culture of adding features and services arises and grows over time, rather than a culture of looking at what's essential to keep providing value to the customer. The crux of a well-designed business is a deep understanding of that business's customer. Again, this sounds fundamental, but I've asked this question of hundreds of CEOs over the last several years – "Who is your customer?" - and rarely receive an answer that signals a rich knowledge of the end user of their products or services.

This is not to say that companies don't have an understanding of who their customer is. However, what I've seen is that this knowledge has often been diluted over time and buried under layers of extras, such as new features or services that were once considered valuable but don't offer any value today.

The concept of designing a business around the customer is not only relevant to a consumer-orientated business. The principle applies just as aptly to a B2B business if we view the business who is buying the product as the customer. The firm selling to the business needs a deep understanding of that business's needs and how to provide value to them. This book focuses on both.

In business we often spend considerable amounts of time, energy and money getting our products right and looking at brand or company values. However, a well-designed business goes beyond the

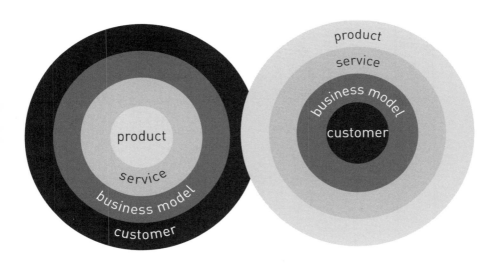

- Product Centric to a *Customer Centric* organisation

product or the quality or the branding. It aligns all aspects around a common point – the customer – and delivers consistently.

Good design upsets the status quo of an established company and often results in ceasing doing things rather than adding more. I speak with many CEOs who tell me they simply don't have the time to stop, take a good look at their business and take stock, so they continue to do more of the same without questioning the value in what they currently offer and how they work. It takes courage to stop!

Becoming design led is about the journey rather than the destination. Today's CEOs have options, and embarking on the Design Led Innovation journey isn't for every CEO or every business. DLI doesn't replace other methods of innovation, such as lean or continuous improvement. If a firm becomes design led it will enhance its lean innovation activities anyway, as "lean" indicates that everything a company does gives their customer value. This is the jumping off point for Design Led Innovation and the entire organisation starts by being explicit about this. This will become clearer in the coming chapters, which show that DLI can't be treated as a discrete event and it can't be delegated. The whole business and its business model needs to be in focus to achieve the benefits of embarking on this journey.

How does a CEO know if the Design Led Innovation journey is the one for their company? Three vital questions hold the key, which all layers of an organisation need to be able to clearly and constantly answer.

If a CEO can't answer these questions clearly and succinctly, it is

1. Who is my customer and what problem am I solving for them?

2. What business activities across the organisation are carried out on a daily basis, which ensure we are focused on addressing our customer's issues?

3. What could I do less of that does not directly address my customer's problems?

likely other members of the organisation are also not able to provide a suitable response and therefore elements of the organisation will most likely be 'poorly designed.' The Design Led Innovation process is a proven approach to increase top-line growth in today's uncertain economic conditions, but will require firms to invest time, energy and resources to ensure that all aspects of the company align to a deep understanding of the company and the customer they are serving.

" It takes coura

e to *STOP!*

Are We There Yet?

who is *sam bucolo?*

This is my first book, which is kind of strange for an academic with 20 years' experience. I've written plenty of conference and journal articles, which are geared towards an academic community. My engagement with industry however, has often been at the coalface where theoretical books offer limited value. To get to this position of respect with industry, I've had an academic career which wasn't fully planned and one could say, isn't typical of the careers of my colleagues.

My background is in industrial design, starting life as a student of design back in a time when industrial design in Australia was not well understood or common. I was the first person in my family to attend university, so embarking on a higher level of learning in an unknown discipline was particularly daunting. However, this also gave me the freedom to explore, as there were no defined boundaries to what was right or wrong in terms of study habits or practice standards. Looking back at my early days of study it felt like I had the authority to challenge and to define my own career trajectory, as there were few job ads for industrial designers, even though our skills and knowledge were in high demand.

For the first few years of my professional life I worked as a design consultant, being asked to design everything from chairs to mobile phones to quite advanced medical devices. The work was interesting and the learning curve was steep. However, as I became more comfortable with my expertise as a designer in being able to solve the problems presented to me, I came to realise that I was often getting the wrong brief from the client. Moreover, I wasn't in a position to change their mindset as I didn't speak their language. I was also surprised to discover how little value firms placed on what the design process could offer their business beyond just designing products.

With my training in design, I was frustrated that companies couldn't conceptualise their business models. Why did they prefer technology-based research and development over intangibles such as a good customer experience? I could see the untapped potential in applying design techniques to the business model, with the customer at its centre. I knew the system was inherently flawed and I wanted to change it. However, at the time it felt like I didn't have the support of many of my colleagues, the design community or most importantly firms, as good design generally equated to a good product design.

This led me to the start of my academic career with further study at a Masters and PhD level, which provided me with a better understanding of the design process and how it can be explored beyond product design. To achieve my goal of changing the system, I knew I needed to constantly span the academic and industry divide to ensure my teaching and research was relevant and applied. As a junior lecturer I undertook several short term projects in industry, and was the first to make myself available for industry-focused projects and opportunities.

Over the last several years Design Led Innovation has become my passion and specialty. I've worked with companies of all sizes and from all sectors along with government to revolutionise business models. I've led several industry initiated research projects and been heavily involved in an industry/university research centre, the *Australian CRC for Interaction Design (ACID)*, as their R&D Director. This allowed me to work with leading firms and global brands as they adopted new interactive technologies to enhance their competitive strategies. It became clear through this work that while companies were able to conceptualise new products and services, the sticking point was aligning this conceptualisation to their business models. This meant that time and time again, projects fell significantly below expectation or failed completely.

While I was working at *ACID*, I led a team, which generated a piece of Intellectual Property that took gaming into hospitals to improve the lives of sick kids. Today, gaming technology is a huge business and an everyday part of medicine. It's the science behind innovations such as simulations used in health education and apps and games to allow patients to monitor their own vital signs. But in 2006, merging gaming and health was a revolutionary concept and I knew this piece of IP had great potential that would most likely not be realised in an academic environment as the idea needed a business to be designed around it.

So in a "eureka" moment, I realised this was the perfect opportunity to get hands-on experience in what I'd been witnessing in companies and what came very naturally to me: stop designing the product and focus on designing the business to enable this great idea to be realised.

I'd designed what I modestly considered a brilliant medical device concept … now I was going to be part of a team to design a business to spin out that product. Rather than undertake further studies, such as an MBA, my practical nature knew that creating a spin-out company was the right way to best understand the role of design and business.

As I embarked on this new chapter of my professional development, I centred everything I could on DLI principles (although the term Design Led Innovation hadn't yet been coined!). As well as gaining invaluable experience in how DLI could truly benefit a company, I came to understand and deeply respect the other challenges that CEOs face every day as I learnt the nitty-gritty of being a leader in a successful, global business.

Ultimately, I knew my destiny was not to be a CEO. I left the company armed with a deep understanding of running a business, a swag of transferrable skills and practical knowledge of how successful Design Led Innovation could be. I came back to an academic life and started working with existing SMEs and large organisations to change their business models from being product or service focused, to customer-centric, using what I had just learnt. But as an academic, I was fortunate enough to be in a position to be able to continue to study this and build up this model of what is now known as Design Led Innovation. This has since been explored and adopted by hundreds of firms around the world.

What I have learnt is that it's difficult to retrofit a DLI approach to an existing firm, but it can most certainly be done. The start-up culture has definitely expanded in recent years and design has had a role in establishing new ventures. But it will be established businesses, in particular SMEs who are the workhorses of the economy, that need to adopt innovation practices to remain relevant in a rapidly changing world.

I've been fortunate to stand side by side with many companies as they take what is a long and often fraught journey to transform through Design Led Innovation. Yes, it's a difficult journey, but the rewards are commensurate with the pain!

Working with business from this position of trust has been an absolute honour and has allowed me to continue to redefine the role of an academic. Ultimately my biggest challenge is yet to come - redefining a future business model for universities - but this can wait for my next book.

Are We There Yet?

acknowledgements

In building this body of work over several years, there are many people who need to be acknowledged and thanked.

Firstly, Dr Cara Wrigley and Dr Judy Mathews, who were my two original academic colleagues. They believed in this approach and came on the journey with me to build up the necessary evidence with industry. Looking back, those early days when we were building something completely new were some of the hardest times I had encountered in my career, but having Cara and Judy around to explore new ways of working with firms and new theories on design and management practices has allowed me to get to where I am today.

Thanks, also, to the firms who were part of the original pilot Government funded programme – *Ulysses*. Their initial belief in the methods, tools – and in me – has allowed me to continue to build up the Design Led Innovation model, from which other firms are now reaping the benefits. Many of the CEOs have become long lasting friends and we continue to challenge each other today.

Some of the case studies I've used in this book have come from other firms I haven't worked with directly, but who have begun their DLI journey working in related programmes. I have met with these leaders through a number of reports and studies I have undertaken, specifically the *Design for Manufacturing Report Study*[1] and the *Design Thinking For Export and Competitiveness Programme*[2], which were supported by the Commonwealth Government of Australia. The lessons I have learnt during this research have been invaluable and have helped me tremendously to shape my thinking in supporting SMEs.

Thanks to Peter King from *CSIRO* who helped me co-author a number of reports, but has become more of a kindred spirit over the past few years to help bring the concept of DLI to our largest scientific-based organisation and into industry government policy.

I acknowledge the kindness and vision of the many Academic and Industry colleges who have given up their time to build an international community around the concept of design for business. The international perspective we have shared from Finland, Italy, Denmark, UK, China and New Zealand reinforces that Design Led Innovation has a wide-reaching application and is not geographically isolated.

To my team at the *UTS Design Innovation research centre*, who have provided me with a new context and platform to build up my research, thank you!

Accolades to Patrick Forrest from my research centre who has used his creative genius to develop the layout for this book. The process of designing this book has helped shape this as a conversation.

To the many reviewers of the early drafts for this book, you know who you are - thanks. Your comments and motivation to encourage me to continue to write and build on initial drafts have been critical in shaping this final version.

Finally, my heartfelt thanks to my family, my wife Lisa and two sons Nathan and Mathew, who have heard countless stories of dad ranting on about the opportunities of design for business. Without your unconditional support and constantly grounding me back into reality, none of this would have been possible – thank you!

let's start.

CHAPTER 1
can you tell me how innovative you are?

can you tell me how innovative you are?

In all the years I've been working with firms, rarely do I hear from them that they're not innovative or lacking ideas. Of course firms are innovative – because innovation can be defined in so many ways the term has become meaningless. From what I've observed in the firms I have worked with, innovation generally equates to busyness and this busyness is what prevents CEOs from asking the tough questions, such as, "Are my innovation efforts helping my business grow?" The saying, "I only have time to work in my business and not on my business," rings true.

However, innovation is the lifeblood of a firm succeeding in uncertain times and most CEOs understand this. Getting them to understand and adopt a model of innovation which is relevant to them is the difficult part. So when I'm having my first conversation with a firm, I often start with a bold statement ... **I do not believe that you are innovative.**

Naturally, this creates some unrest in the room. CEOs will often defend their business by rattling off multiple projects they're undertaking.

Usually, these have been well-considered and managed. They point to sales associated with key innovations in the market and also talk at length about the process (and costs) around protecting their idea through various intellectual property mechanisms. They are proud of the awards they've been given for a particular innovation, which externally validates that they must be innovative.

So to have someone, especially an academic, challenge their level of innovation doesn't sit comfortably with most. After listening to their defence of current innovation practices, I qualify my statement and ask the question again … Are all your innovation efforts relevant to today's changing economic conditions and helping your future customers through this transition?

I've found firms struggle to answer this as it forces them to question some of the fundamentals of their business. They may not be in distress and have no need to question what has been successful in the past. Given the shifts we've experienced in our economic reality, one would expect their customer's needs would also change and the firm must also respond to this through innovation.

Moving beyond incremental improvements which focus on today's business will only occur if companies have a fresh view of who their future customer is and what problems they will be solving for them. Understanding this change and more importantly acting on this change is the difficult task.

To be clear, the economic shifts to which businesses have had to respond to ensure they remain competitive and relevant have been significant. Globally, this has been driven from structural economic shifts, which have resulted in fundamental changes to capital markets and impacted collectively on business and society across most nations. How individual governments and nations have reacted to these changes is well outside the scope of this book, other than to say that one of the drivers of change is supporting businesses in how they compete

"I do not believe you are innovative or asked another way... Are all your innovation efforts relevant to today's changing economic conditions and helping your future customers through this transition?"

through innovation, as their growth directly correlates on a nation's standard of living.

In Australia we managed our global financial crisis through a combination of measures. One measure was to support SMEs to remain globally competitive through innovation.

Various reports have estimated that the number of Australian SMEs make up over 95 per cent of businesses in Australia and 33 precent of its Gross Domestic Product (GDP). From these studies. this compares to over 85 per cent of businesses in the US, and nearly 95 percent of businesses in the UK. In Australia, prior to the Global Financial Crisis (GFC) we experienced twenty years of uninterrupted economic growth, vastly improving our living standards. This mainly came from a low Australian dollar and the commodity boom driven by our resources sector. However, the GFC has altered this economic equation and Australia can no longer rely on the resources sector to provide the foundation for growth. Additionally, Australia is now considered a high cost environment and not protected from imports as it was in the past.

Other nations have supported their own economies with other strategies and SMEs are often the recipient of these policy interventions. However, many of these support programmes could be thought of as incremental business tweaks or productivity enhancements, which provide an immediate bottom line benefit to the firm. The economic changes we have witnessed require a rethink of support programmes and Design Led Innovation addresses this gap.

In Australia, several studies have reported and identified a decline in our manufacturing sector and that our competitiveness has been deteriorating over the last several years. Other nations face their own challenges with their sectors disappearing. We need to do something! The SME sector is at a crossroads. On one hand SMEs have lower start-up costs and are nimble due to their size; on the other, the challenges outlined above make it difficult for them to grow to meet demand. The imperative to increase the success of SMEs is clear.

Competition is now global and businesses have no choice but to measure their competitiveness against the world's best or risk being undercut. Technology is enabling entirely new business models to develop and evolve rapidly. Demographic changes are reshaping patterns of demand, labour force participation and labour mobility. As emerging economies continue to invest and develop, they will move up the value chain, increasingly competing with advanced economies to offer sophisticated and specialised services.

I've presented this brave new world to hundreds of SMEs, during workshops and forums over the last several years. Many CEOs are acutely aware of the formidable challenges they face and are daunted by the prospect of attaining growth in a new economic reality. Their fear is often not knowing where to start.

To help firms start to answer the question of how relevant DLI is to them, I get them to look at their business from a customer-centred perspective, which is the starting point of a design led approach. I ask them three important questions.

1. Who is your customer and what problem are you solving for them?

2. What business activities across the organisation do you carry out on a daily basis, which ensure you're addressing your customer's problems?

3. What could you do less of that does not directly address your customer's problems?

On the surface these three questions seem quite harmless and straightforward, but when firms are asked to provide the evidence to support their answers, most have struggled.

Most CEOs can answer the first question, but often their description of their customer is defined in terms of product features and specifications and not a problem the firm is trying to solve for their customer. Having this empathetic or customer-centric view of their customer is the critical part of any business and is the first step to becoming design led. (Chapter 2 focuses on this in more detail.) Design is core to building this understanding of the customer beyond a functional description, to one that builds empathy and frames their issues and wider concerns.

The second question then gets to the heart of how a business aligns its core processes, activities and staff to address the customer problem. If a firm can describe their customer in a broader way than a functional description of their needs, the scope for innovation expands and it quickly becomes clear that the entire organisation has a role to solve these problems … such as the way accounts are managed, how the company works with distributors and solving any issues with the supply chain and logistics. To lead by design, every aspect of a

"Who is your customer and what problem are you solving for them?

What business activities across the organisation do you carry out on a daily basis, which ensure you're addressing your customer's problems?

What could you do less of that does not directly address your customer's problems?"

successful business must and should be defined around an empathetic view of their customer.

I've found that most firms struggle most with the last question, "What could you do less of that does not directly address your customer's problems?" Once the customer and their needs have been identified, a firm needs to take an objective view of what activities (for example departments, innovation programmes, products and services) the company no longer needs or could be redeployed.

I often hear that firms are too busy to innovate and they don't have enough hours in the day to look at another innovation programme. Innovation can also involve taking away activities to simplify a business structure. Ensuring that everything and everyone in the organisation aligns to the understanding of the customer is the foundation of leading by design. However to do this, firms need to open up their thinking to see innovation as more than just something new that requires time and resources. It often requires *stopping* something, something that may no longer be adding value to a customer.

I regularly see firsthand that innovation inside SMEs is not usually framed around simplifying a business and stopping certain activities. What I often hear back from firms is that these activities are too difficult to stop and in most cases they may be cash flow positive. In the long term, they may be detrimental to the business as they are not providing any real value to the customer.

These three questions get to the heart of Design Led Innovation. The first question forces the firm to expand its understanding of who its customer is and what current problems the company is solving for them. Having this customer centric view will allow for divergent thinking within the organisation and will enable new ideas and opportunities to emerge. The last two questions form the second aspect of how design can assist a business to innovate. Design isn't just about coming up with new ideas. Design is very much about getting to an outcome and ensuring the solution is refined, elegant and purposeful. To achieve this the firm must also adopt a divergent and convergent thinking mindset to ensure everything it does can be directly related back to

- Convergent Thinking Mindset

a customer value proposition.

I illustrate this to a CEO by asking them to think of a well designed product they've recently bought. The response is often a tangible product and more often than not a car. I ask them to describe why they purchased this product and I ask what problem they were trying to solve with it. They rarely describe it in terms of its functionality and they often speak about the emotional pleasures of driving. I then ask them to describe the integration of the features of this product around how it meets their needs. They describe in great detail how the vehicle performs, they talk about its dynamics and stability, and relate this to body styling, materials, surface finish, dashboard layout and interior configuration, relating this back to driving performance and experience. Depending on the brand they recount their positive experience with having the car serviced and how this adds to the driving pleasure and their all round satisfaction with their purchase. What the CEO has done is refer to a solution, which meets their needs at an experiential level and that all features of this product and the business model have been resolved and integrated. In other words, the entire product is well designed.

Then comes the hard part ... I ask them to describe their business in the same way. I ask them to describe their customer's experience and how each of the element of their business relates to this. This is when they struggle.

Becoming design led is not just about designing products or services, but taking an entire look at the business from a customer perspective and redesigning all elements from this understanding. This is not a linear process, but one that requires many iterations and prototyping with customers and staff.

Centor[1] is a wonderful illustration of how a firm has looked at the process of design, applied this to their entire business and made some challenging decisions as a result of this process.

Nigel Spork took over his family's business *Centor* in 1997. Founded in Brisbane, Australia in 1951 by his Grandfather Frank, it manufactured hardware for windows and doors. Now, *Centor* is a multi award winning manufacturer of innovative doors and windows, employing 180 staff, with regional headquarters in the US, UK, Poland and China. It had experienced 30 per cent growth for 10 consecutive years when it embarked on a radical reinvention prompted by the GFC.

I worked with *Centor* as they agreed to look at themselves through the DLI lens. As you would imagine, the first challenge I set Nigel was to identify *Centor's* customer. This proved to be the first of many frank exchanges between Nigel and me. I'd been doing my own research and knew that the question, who is your customer, would prove controversial.

Nigel thought the question was a no-brainer. After nearly 60 years in business, *Centor* had assumed they had a deep knowledge of who their customer was and what they wanted from their products. To prove his point, he asked his eight executives who their customer was, and was absolutely blown away to receive eight different answers. He couldn't understand how this was possible.

Nigel and his team took a deep dive into their customer's world and so was born the persona (a fictional character which the firm can use to embody the characteristics of their customer), 'Wendy'. She was a homeowner looking to do a new build in which she would be closely involved. For the next year, *Centor* undertook 300 interviews around the world to learn not only about Wendy's expectations and motivations, but also about their channel to market – their business partners, the architects, builders and dealers. Nigel and his team realised they had to solve different problems for Wendy and for others in the channel. In the process, they discovered their channel to market was a mess.

Nigel asked his senior leadership team if *Centor* could become 10 times bigger if it carried on doing the same thing - the answer was a firm no. This was because their products were easily copied and patents not always effective. Nigel had a light bulb moment when he was allowed to peer inside other successful businesses as a business competition awards judge. He saw many companies growing at between 8 and 15 per cent … but one that had changed its business model was growing at 400 per cent. Nigel realised that to achieve this kind of growth, *Centor* would have to reinvent itself and this meant moving into designing and manufacturing windows and doors, rather than just making door components. This shift offered an opportunity for the kind of growth Nigel envisaged and also to provide value back to their customer Wendy.

Nigel knew this reinvention would be an expensive investment, so he asked his team which of *Centor*'s 181 research projects could be cancelled to free up manpower and money. The answer was none. So Nigel – taking on the role of the Disruptor, which I'll explain later - cancelled all 181 and led his team on a 15 month journey to work out the company's purpose, identify their customer and create a viable business model.

This journey wasn't always a happy one. Nigel says the company went down some frightening, dark alleys. A good example was when *Centor* invested heavily in machinery to create a fibreglass product for one of their most lucrative export markets. The trouble was, further exploration of their customer revealed that "Wendy" didn't want fibreglass … she wanted a high end product and was willing to pay for it. The investment wasn't wasted. In hindsight, Nigel can see the value of this fail fast model, as a new approach to experimentation has now been adopted throughout the company. Although it was a brutal lesson, this experience brought home to Nigel that in the design process, everything is referenced from a customer perspective. We all know that being caught up in a daily routine can blind us from perspective.

Centor is starting to reap the benefits of its redesign, with its product development plan locked in for a five year period. After identifying its customer and designing a product to meet her needs, *Centor* launched its ground breaking new product, the Integrated Door, at the Grand Designs show in the UK in October 2013. The response was overwhelming, with agreement from thousands of customers that

Centor has created the best door system in the world. *Centor's* staff feel they have solved unsolvable problems and achieved a breakthrough. The orders and financial rewards are following.

I love *Centor's* story. I admit it was difficult challenging Nigel and his company, so thoroughly and consistently. Nigel says I would come in periodically and ask confronting and challenging questions and would sit there nodding and smiling, knowing that he knew the answer and didn't like it, but it was time to face up to it. He rose to the challenges, and brought his whole company with him. Sure it was uncomfortable, but he doesn't regret a minute of any of it because the outcomes are worth it.

The key lesson from *Centor's* story is that the starting point was not a company in distress - *Centor* was far from that - but the CEO needed to be challenged about how they undertook innovation and for whom. Many CEOs indicate they are rarely challenged on what they do. Design allows for this conversation to be started.

The second key learning was that by asking the three questions: Who is your customer and what problem are you solving for them? What business activities across the organisation do you carry out on a daily basis, which ensure you're addressing your customer's problems? And what could you do less of that does not directly address your customer's problems? forced the entire organisation to rethink how it could provide value to its customer.

Without the leadership provided by the CEO, this depth of company renewal could not have been achieved. Likewise, if Nigel hadn't brought all his staff along on the journey, by building a common understanding of their customer and allowing staff to make decisions about how they could provide value to the customer, *Centor's* new business model would have remained a great idea and never been put into practice. Leading by design allows for both activities to be undertaken and is critical for a firm's future success.

Throughout this book I'll share the stories of some of the companies that I've worked with like *Centor* and who have generously given me their time, energy and insights. These case studies will illustrate that becoming design led is a journey and it's the mindset that the CEO and then the entire company takes on this journey, which is the critical path. There is no how to manual, but a CEO can feel confident that reflecting on how these principles and concepts can be applied to their own business, will extend their innovation efforts.

Are We There Yet?

?

Before reading further, business owners should ask themselves if their own innovation efforts are relevant to today and if their entire business provides value to their customer. The hardest part of answering this question is: how does a business owner really know? When was the last time they stopped to ask … and listen?

It's not just CEOs who need to ask confronting questions. Anyone supporting an organisation in their innovation efforts such as employees, consultants or designers, should look at that company, try to map each of their activities to a customer value proposition and highlight how many gaps there are inside the organisation. How would they frame this insight to the CEO of the organisation to start the conversation to get them to rethink their business?

notes...

notes...

this should be sent to the design and marketing department

this should be sent to the design and marketing department

While running hundreds of introductory workshops for companies on how to lead by design, a constant refrain from CEOs I often hear is, "I have a design department and don't need this capability" or "I know my customer because I have a great sales team". I also hear from staff inside firms, in particular the design related staff, who say "I feel stuck in my current role as designer... we don't seem to be having the impact we could have for our companies."

I'm of the firm belief that the word "design" gets in the way when thinking about new models of innovation within a company. However, discarding the word entirely would take away the richness and history in its meaning. Therefore, I have persevered with the word 'design'. This chapter will focus on how firms have come to realise a new meaning of the word design and its value to their business.

Design, like innovation, has multiple meanings; too many to mention in this book. Outside of academia and the design profession, I often hear it described as what a firm produces or sells, or as the department within an organisation responsible for the development of its products and services. So when I present myself to a firm to talk about leading by design, I am often directed to the head of design or someone who has assumed this responsibility. Sure I can have a great conversation with this person, but often the conversation focuses on, "yeah it would be great to get design valued differently around here ... if only the firm understood what we did."

Are We There Yet?

When I first started running programmes for companies to introduce Design Led Innovation, they were referred to as "building design capability" workshops. This made sense to me, as this is what I was hoping to achieve - to build design capability in all staff (not just the design department) to get them to understand their customer and align all business functions around this meaning. This narrow view meant that the workshops were perceived as only being needed by companies that didn't have a design department. The irony was that firms who did have a design department and relied on them as the core source of innovation were the ones who were most at risk and they needed a shift in their approach to innovation. (I'll come back to this point later.)

I started to rename the workshops to focus more on customer centricity and designing around the customer. This still didn't have the desired impact but at least it resonated more with companies. Now, CEOs saw framing the problem as a marketing one and started sending their marketing teams along who were armed with reams of paper, which precisely articulated their market segmentation and customer profiles. When I asked the marketing staff how this information translated to strategy and decision making in all aspects of their business, the common refrain was that this was not their responsibility and was outside of their scope of influence – this was the CEO's responsibility. Their role was to collect data and more often than not, their method of market research was backward looking and about justifying market segmentation, rather than forward looking and about understanding future customer problems.

The people I needed in the room were a mix of these roles: the CEO or owner of the firm who was ultimately responsible for the entire operations of the business; the head of marketing (if that role existed); and ideally the head of the design department or engineering team (again, if that role existed). For a small business, this was a big ask but it was something that I began to insist on to ensure that the barriers of business could be broken down together.

Getting these leaders in the room to start to collectively look at the business was a vital first step. It allowed me to highlight what I often see as a critical problem faced by business. As I stated in Chapter 1, alignment of business activities across an organisation against a clear definition of its customer is the core of Design Led Innovation.

However, getting an organisation to understand that there's little or no consistency in the understanding of the company's strategy and customer is no easy task. Only by being brave and asking the question and by answering it honestly, can the firm start to reveal – and understand – the issue of disconnection within their company.

What I've found is that there are a number of different techniques and approaches, which have helped to start this conversation and get the firms on the journey to becoming design led. I'll share these through four different case studies, which I hope will inspire the start of conversations within companies.

Rinstrum[1] is a quintessential Australian SME set up in 1992, making components for the weighing industry. I have worked with

"Put senior leadership in one room and ask them what the company's strategy is and why it was developed and there will be as many answers as there are people in the room."

Darren Pearson, who joined them in 1995 as a design engineer, bought into the business with co-partner Paul Cooper in 2005 and became their CEO. *Rinstrum* now has sales revenues of 10 times those of 1995 and enjoys global reach with a manufacturing facility in Sri Lanka and sales hubs in Australia, Germany and the US. This is the kind of growth and success that can happen when a company starts by admitting there is a problem and Design Led Innovation was a catalyst to start this conversation.

Darren was ambitious to expand and move beyond manufacturing components. The company was innovative, had a good engineering design department, and had been successful to date. Their customers at the time wanted generic components so they could easily swap suppliers, leaving *Rinstrum* with business model that offered little differentation. Darren understood this, but his leadership team didn't. That was problem one. Problem two was that Darren realised that the only way to overcome their risky manufacturing strategy was to move to becoming a solutions based company; that meant potentially going into competition with elements of their supply chain. Both of these problems, Darren told me when we met, were daunting, and would be very confronting for his staff, as they were not often aware of the complexity of the business outside of their own functional areas. When these kinds of discussions had been broached previously at *Rinstrum*, they stopped quickly because the challenges were overwhelming. Darren found himself at a crossroads. He had multiple ideas of possible directions for where the company could go,

but where to start to the conversation with staff and make structural changes to the business was the sticking point.

Darren signed up *Rinstrum* to a government run Design Innovation programme and then ongoing mentoring with me. Ultimately, this programme helped reveal to him and his staff the real issues *Rinstrum* was facing and to put strategies in place to resolve them. Darren rose to all of my challenges and his courage and leadership allowed the business to transition to leading by design without pressing the self-destruct button.

The first activity of the programme was to highlight the gaps across the management team by letting staff collectively undertake a customer "deep dive". Staff were given a framework to talk to end users about their problems and shown how to listen and interpret key insights. However, what they collectively found was that the information they were hearing was often contradictory from the different stakeholders in their supply chain. Designers know the best problems are when there are contradictions, and *Rinstrum* found itself facing a huge one – how to add value across its entire organisation without cannibalising its existing business?

Given that the management group now realised the magnitude of the challenge, it was clear that the solution would not be a new product offering or a tweak of their existing systems, but a complete redesign of their business model.

Therefore, they needed to reassess their entire value proposition and prototype different business models and operating models, while continuing to learn with their customers. This was a whole of company activity led by Darren, with key staff hearing firsthand what the problems were and where there could be tradeoffs. When everyone across the organisation understood this, *Rinstrum* was in the position to provide integrated solutions to meet varied customer needs.

One of the customers that *Rinstrum* started talking to were farmers, as the company provided weighing solutions to the agriculture sector. To understand the problem farmers faced, *Rinstrum* would normally rely on insights from their distributors, but now staff were being asked to go and speak with the end user directly. The *Rinstrum* team discovered that farmers who owned their own trucks needed to ensure they did not drive overloaded. The chain of responsibility meant that the entire enterprise, which the farmers were responsible for, was at risk if there was an accident with an overloaded truck, not to mention the cost of fines. *Rinstrum* hadn't realised this was a problem as they had only provided solutions further upstream when the product was being unloaded. *Rinstrum* set about solving the problem from the farmers' perspective, by designing an innovative solution - an axle scale that is dropped into a hole in the ground at the farm gate. When the truck drives over it, the weight registers.

The farmers loved it, but as with most great solutions often there is a knock on effect somewhere in the supply chain and one of their key partners was not interested in this solution as it impacted on how they currently served the farmer. The main challenge for *Rinstrum* with the axle scale design was that our traditional channel to market to the product design, allowing the farmers to install and service the product themselves with no special knowledge or tools.

Rinstrum could have retreated and not gone further with helping the farmer, but by having multiple staff from within the organisation work on this problem, a new business model and technical solutions could be developed. The big takeaway for Rinstrum on applying Design Led Innovation was the integration of business strategy and product design using the same tools and techniques.

Normally when this type of problem presented itself at *Rinstrum*, the difficult questions would have been avoided. Darren and everyone in his company, now look at the world from a completely different perspective. They've embedded prototyping in all areas of the business, not just prototyping new products, but intangibles such as new business models to get through these difficult conversations.

Rinstrum's story illustrates that aligning the business strategy to the end user is difficult but achievable. The whole process can be quite disruptive, requires a new mindset and is in many ways counterintuitive. Darren told us he really had to fight his instinct to get quick results, but that slowing down the process and seeing the problem firsthand from multiple customer perspectives proved more efficient in the long run.

He's also completely changed the way he views design. In the past, the company had a list of tasks that centred on the design process. Now, they always start with a user story that says, "As a user of that product their problem is…" This becomes the project brief

"Aligning a business strategy to the end user is difficult but achievable ... the whole process can be quite disruptive, requires a new mindset and is in many ways counterintuitive, as the instinct will be to constantly try to get quick results ... but slowing down the process is more efficient in the long run."

and is no longer just a series of product specifications. To achieve this shift in thinking, they undertake short design projects centred on understanding what the user's problem is that needs to be solved; rather than committing to an entire business case or research and development programme with a critical path analysis that doesn't allow for changes to be made once they learn more about the customer problem. Now, if the initial prototyping process shows up a challenge, it's quick and easy to review the direction and not compromise on providing an integrated solution.

Earlier in this chapter I discussed how a key part of the design led journey is getting firms to reframe how they see design. Sure, *Rinstrum* has a design department with some very talented designers. But design, as applied to business, is different. And yes, they have a sales team with a strong track record, but that doesn't mean a company knows its customer.

Design Led Innovation in the *Rinstrum* context was shifting their perspective about design to focus on understanding customers before they started building technical solutions or making a sale. Through the process of prototyping with their customers, they are now able to reframe what the real problem is and provide both technical solutions and a business model, integrating several partners without compromise.

This isn't always easy, but at least the framework and mindset have been embedded inside *Rinstrum* to allow decisions to be made.

As shown in the *Rinstrum* case study, business leaders shouldn't be daunted by the word "design". And designers shouldn't be held back by what they think "design" can provide. It's a small word, but with many different components. Each has a different role and a different value. A useful description I often use comes from the *Cox Report*, which was a UK review of design. It outlines the difference between creativity, innovation and design.

What I like about this definition is that it can speak to an entire organisation. As I mentioned earlier, rarely do I go into a firm where creativity is an issue; however, most firms will not describe themselves as creative. Staff generally know what the issues are and know of solutions to address them. What I often see is that these solutions are too narrow, as they have come from a single departmental perspective; or they're not aligned to company strategy; or the solutions require major change within the organisation. In the *Cox Report* definition, design can be seen as the glue which enables a firm's creativity to be explored - not just the process, which enables a firm to get to solutions quickly and efficiently. This is essentially what has occurred at *Rinstrum*.

CREATIVITY

IS THE GENERATION OF NEW IDEAS – EITHER NEW WAYS OF LOOKING AT EXISTING PROBLEMS, OR OF SEEING NEW OPPORTUNITIES, PERHAPS BY EXPLOITING EMERGING TECHNOLOGIES OR CHANGES IN MARKETS.

INNOVATION

IS THE SUCCESSFUL EXPLOITATION OF NEW IDEAS. IT IS THE PROCESS THAT CARRIES THEM THROUGH TO NEW PRODUCTS, NEW SERVICES, NEW WAYS OF RUNNING THE BUSINESS OR EVEN NEW WAYS OF DOING BUSINESS.

DESIGN

IS WHAT LINKS CREATIVITY AND INNOVATION. IT SHAPES IDEAS TO BECOME PRACTICAL AND ATTRACTIVE PROPOSITIONS FOR USERS OR CUSTOMERS. DESIGN MAY BE DESCRIBED AS CREATIVITY DEPLOYED TO A SPECIFIC END. [2]

- The Cox Review of Creativity in Business

Are We There Yet?

Another approach I use to help firms overcome this blockage around the meaning of design and where it sits within the organisation, is the *Danish Design Ladder*[3]. This was developed by the *Danish Design Centre (DDC)* in 2003 as a tool to measure the level of design activity in businesses. The Ladder was used initially as a framework for a survey on how Danish firms were adopting design.

The first survey was in 2003 and was repeated in 2007, with the aim of assessing the economic benefits of design. The *Danish Design Ladder* provides an assessment of how many companies actually moved up a rung on the ladder over the course of four years.

danish design ladder [3]

STAGE 1: NO DESIGN
No tangible approach to design within a firm.

STAGE 2: DESIGN AS STYLING
Design is relevant in aesthetic considerations such as style, appearance and ergonomics.

STAGE 3: DESIGN AS PROCESS
Design is considered as a process or method in product or service output, only embedded in the initial stages of development. The design solution is procured externally and is adapted to the requirements of the end-user using a multidisciplinary approach.

STAGE 4: DESIGN AS BUSINESS STRATEGY
Design is integral to the company's continuous renewal of their business concept as a means of encouraging innovation. Process is fused with the company's key objectives and plays a role at every stage of development.

STEP 6:
DESIGN AS NATIONAL
COMPETITIVE
STRATEGY

The role of design
to transform entire
sectors

STEP 5:
DESIGN AS COMMUNITY
AND ORGANISATIONAL
TRANSFORMATION

Design of the organis-
ational structure and
business model

STEP 4:
DESIGN AS A
BUSINESS STRATEGY

Design is an integral
part of the company's
business strategy

STEP 3:
DESIGN AS AN
INNOVATION PROCESS

Design is an integral
part of the company's
innovation process

STEP 2:
DESIGN AS STYLING

Design is used for
styling and finishing
of company products

STEP 1:
NON-DESIGN

This company does
not use design
systematically

- extended *Danish Design Ladder*

The original *Danish Design Ladder* stops at 'design as a business strategy'. From my work with SMEs, I have adapted it by adding two more steps—'design as organisational transformation,' which refers to the redesign of the entire organisational structure and business model of the organisation; and 'design as national competitive strategy, 'which refers to the role of design to transform entire sectors to ensure a nation remains competitive and prosperous. These two additional steps allow for a more complete description of the way the multiple layers of design can be deployed by organisations in completely new ways to ensure they remain competitive and prosperous.

The ladder is helpful as it shows how firms currently understand design and helps them to acknowledge other applications, which they may not have explored. However, I have also seen how the ladder is misinterpreted as a series of sequential steps that firms must progress through; and when firms identify where they are on the ladder, they believe the gap is too big to bridge to a new step. So I prefer to use the ladder to map how a firm currently perceives design, which is often not well understood by everyone in the organisation. I use this as a starting point to show different approaches and outcomes of how design can be applied, which can often be undertaken in parallel.

In my experience, most companies who are seeking to embark on a design led journey are at Stage Two of the ladder and this is where they get stuck. I'd like to share the story of *Gourmet Garden*[4], where I used the ladder as a means of shifting this firm's understanding of design and how they pushed through to Stages Three, Four and Five and reaped the benefits from this journey.

When I first met *Gourmet Garden,* it was a successful Australian SME with unique patented technology that specialised in the growing, processing and packaging of fresh herbs and spices into squeezable tubes without heat treatment or preservatives. In just over a decade it had grown to be the global market leader in chilled convenient herbs, distributing to over 20,000 supermarkets in over 15 countries. CEO Nick White took over in 2007 when the company was already quite successful, however, discovered conflicting views about the company's purpose, its competitive advantage and who its customer actually was. Despite its success, even in its most mature market, Australia, they had only been able to capture 15 per cent consumer penetration despite millions of dollars in TV advertising.

The key challenge for Nick was to question what was limiting growth in their business. When looking at this problem from a key customer's point of view, both consumers and chefs articulated that their current product – pastes in tubes – was proving a barrier in terms of functionality and understanding. The product looked interesting on the shelf, but they didn't buy it because they weren't sure what it was or how to use it. Over 3-4 years these issues started to be resolved as a Stage Two design problem - essentially developing a new "chopped" product technology, better packaging and product communication around what he believed was a good understanding of the customer. However, he felt more could be done.

This is how I was introduced to Nick and *Gourmet Garden*, to see if

Design Led Innovation could assist the commericalisation of their 2nd generation technology of pre-prepared chopped herbs. After a series of short meetings and asking the same three questions I presented in Chapter 1, Nick was convinced that a technology focused solution alone was not the answer. The company boldly put a halt to a hasty launch plan and began a process to develop a deeper understanding of their customer.

Through the support of a government based programme, I was part of a team, which was able to work with *Gourmet Garden* as we took a good look at what the company wanted to achieve and how they would address some of the barriers that were stymying further growth. After the programme's completion, Nick engaged me to continue to work with them to address the questions that had arisen during the programme.

Nick and his senior leadership team were pushed to dive deep and develop stories about *Gourmet Garden's* customers. The most obvious place to start was with the end user, who they affectionately named Suzie, a working mother. Other customers who were not normally fully considered were also explored, such as retail partners, chefs and product developers within foodservice/industrial channels. Nick admitted he was skeptical about how this could benefit them; in fact, he said to me, "we thought: why are we going to waste all our time asking them (our customers) about their day? We need to focus on the product issues!"

Instead, Nick was surprised with the richness of the insights that came out of this design led process, which took the company down new paths they had never contemplated. Actually observing professional chefs and ordinary busy cooks in their kitchens; analysing hundreds of shopping trips and everyday fridges. The primary insight was around how busy Suzie was and the struggle the home cook faces every day coming up with something to cook. The key was to understand this challenge so the company could create something to make life easier for the busy cook. Noticing that most chefs had all their ingredients neatly labelled and partitioned, they asked their designers to recreate the '70s dried herb rack and bring it into the 21st century by developing packs that delivered a herb garden to your fingertips in the fridge. Also, most TV chefs seem to have their herbs already washed, chopped and presented in bowls, so the company developed clickable stackable bowl formats too. The new containers proved very attractive to consumers and have won numerous packaging design awards.

The other key design element was around prototyping and failing early. The first exposure of the new, exciting chopped product (which lasts four weeks) in a test kitchen was a disappointment, with consumers not deeming it as fresh but rather semi or lightly dried. Effectively co-designing with consumers had identified "lightly dried" as the most appropriate benchmark descriptor.

These were all good product solutions, which demonstrate the quick results that can be achieved by looking at customers from a different perspective – not asking what they want, but watching what they do and why they do it.

Gourmet Garden's more intuitive understanding of their customers has ensured the successful launch of the new "lightly dried" technology, which is a world first. However, if they'd followed their instincts to rush towards production and launch without delving deeper into the customer's life, Nick believes they would have ended up with a wonderful technology solution, but potentially second rate product solution that may well have missed the mark with consumers.

Nick told me that following a design led approach has enabled the company to understand that design is not just an outcome, it's a way of thinking and an approach that each senior leader in the organisation uses to make business decisions around their customers.

Nick has shifted his approach to design from Stage Two to Stage Five on the *Danish Design Ladder*, but in doing this he needed to build new innovation processes (Stage Three) and strategies (Stage Four). The Design Led Innovation process has opened up their eyes to how you can use design to commercialise new technology around a deep understanding of customers. He will be the first to admit they haven't finished their journey, but equipped with this new way of thinking, he feels the opportunities are endless.

The *Gourmet Garden* case study shows that a firm can use design in multiple ways across the organisation. However, the firm needs to be open to understanding a new application of design. In my experience, this often comes unstuck is if the design department becomes too precious about their role within the organisation and insists they should ultimately be responsible for all things design. When looking at the *Danish Design Ladder*, it becomes clear that design needs to become 'democratised' within an organisation. There are instances when classically trained designers are required (such as in Stage Two and Three), but when it comes to Stages Four and Five, the process requires the whole organisation.

I've explained that DLI can be the foundation of successful change, enabling CEOs to look at their business and customers differently. This kind of systemic change is only possible if the CEO brings the rest of their organisation on board, while managing the expectations of all staff in their current and future roles.

Another approach I have found useful in getting firms to make this shift in how they see design is through the use of the *Doblin Ten Types of Innovation* framework[5].

Doblin is a group of designers, social scientists, engineers, and MBAs who work with clients to build new businesses. Initially developed by *Doblin* in 1998, the *Doblin Ten Types of Innovation* help companies shift their attention from products to business models. The *Doblin* team came to understand that traditionally, executives equated innovation with the development of new products. However, creating new products is only one way to innovate, and on its own, it provides the lowest return on investment and the least competitive advantage. Companies that integrate multiple types of innovation will develop offerings that are more difficult to duplicate and generate higher returns.

Like many others, I've come to use the *Doblin The Ten Types of Innovation* as a valuable resource for firms to shift their understanding of innovation, as it provide provides a useful taxonomy of approaches.

doblin ten types of innovation [5]

CONFIGUATION
Profit Model: *How you make money*
Network: *How you connect wtith others to create value*
Structure: *How you organise and align your talent and assets*
Process: *How you use signatures or superior methods to do your work*

OFFERING
Product Performance: *How you develop distinguishing features and functionality*
Product Systems: *How you create complementary products and services*

EXPERIENCE
Service: *How you support and amplify the value of your offerings*
Channel: *How you deliver your offerings to customers and users*
Brand: *How you represent your offerings and business*
Customer Engagement: *How you foster compelling interactions*

In the following section, I'll highlight how this framework can help shift a firm's perspective on how it perceives the role of innovation and why design is critical. I'll share two stories, where I have retrofitted the *Doblin Ten Types of Innovation* to the firms' innovation process to highlight how valuable this framework can be and what the results can look like.

I was fortunate to establish a university collaboration with iconic German carmaker, *BMW*. During this time *BMW* took a brave and unprecedented approach to innovation and as I was constantly visiting the *BMW* headquarters in Munich, I was able to follow this project firsthand. I've spoken about this elsewhere[6], but would like to retell this story.

BMW wanted to design a new product. So, with CEO support, they started with a cross-functional team to redefine who their customer was, define a new business model and then design a case which supported this. This turned out to be a completely different model to how they'd done things previously. What happened over the next four years illustrates how *BMW* overcame organisational challenges to achieve what *BMW* management called revolutionary change. *BMW* innovated not only in products, but across all *Doblin Ten Types of Innovation*.

Here's how it transpired.

In 2007, *BMW* announced its new strategic objective was to be "the leading provider of premium products and premium services for individual mobility." They wanted to explore what it meant to go from innovating around the concept of efficient dynamics (essentially new vehicles or in the terms of the *Doblin* model 'the offering'), to sustainable mobility (the experience and configuration). Rather than just selling cars, *BMW* wanted to explore the concept of selling mobility and services. This new approach opened up all sorts of possibilities. A hand-picked team of 10 was tasked with 'reshaping the future,' in any form that that would take.

With full CEO and board support, the members of the *"Think Tank Project i"* were taken from their regular jobs and encouraged to question every product and process that currently existed.

Their first step was to sketch out – literally – a vision of what mobility should look like in the future. This didn't start with sketching out a new type of electric car, which they are well equipped to do, but to conceptualise and design a new understanding of how their future customers would remain mobile. This required them to go beyond the vehicle as the primary source of mobility and consider opportunities that seem far removed from an automotive manufacturer in terms of business models, partners and materials. To test some of the assumptions they'd made in the design of this new future, the team developed a prototype, the *MINI E*, of which only 600 were manufactured and delivered to selected customers. Trialled between 2009 and 2012, the *MINI E* showed an electric car could solve issues such as charging time and driving range. As part of this exploration, new services were also explored, again not constrained to the offering as this was not the starting point, but delivering on the experience of what mobility was. For instance, a built-in app for car sharing and finding a parking space or charging point for the customer's electric car, were part of the exploration. This also required design, but the key was that the design brief was linked to a much broader set of customer experiences.

Customers approved enthusiastically. The *BMW Active E*, with a production run of 1000, was tested from 2011, before *BMW* finally launched the *BMW i3* in 2013, with the *BMW i8* following.

BMW didn't just revolutionise product; the *i3* and *i8* also involved a new production process. Instead of a linear movement - press shop to body shop to paint shop to assembly - *BMW* got two assemblies working simultaneously – a drive assembly and a life assembly (involving people). This halved the conventional production time.

After about two and a half years, the team of 10 had grown to over 200 and had successfully kick-started a whole new way of approaching innovation.

The *BMW* example shows how innovation goes beyond the offering and just technology or products (cars). Speaking with members of the team, it was clear that the approach challenged the practice of how they went about 'doing' innovation. The starting point was looking at the future customer experience and then designing a business model to support this. A great car was also developed, but only formed part of the overall offering, supporting the new business model.

In talking with people at *BMW* who worked on this project, there was a real sense of achievement that came with being given the authority to question every part of the business. This could only have been achieved with the highest level of support in the organisation, the CEO. However, even with this support, the team faced a lot of scepticism and questions about why they were considering such diverse solutions.

I'll explore this further in the next chapter, but I wanted to highlight that shifting the thinking of what constitutes innovation inside an organisation is difficult. When there's a culture of thinking that innovation only relates to the development of products, shifting this perspective is one of the greatest tasks to be addressed. If the shift can't be made from focusing on product offering to the experience-configuration types of innovation, as described in the *Doblin Ten Types of Innovation*, design will always remain a subset of the Product Innovation and stuck at Stage Two and Three of the *Danish Design ladder*.

To further illustrate how firms can make this shift, I'll come back to a SME case study. *RØDE Microphones*[7] is a uniquely Australian owned and operated audio company that has a presence in more than 100 countries. Their main hub is in Sydney, with offices in Seattle, Los Angeles, New York and Hong Kong, making *RØDE* a truly global company.

Peter Freedman is the CEO of *RØDE* and he's an inspirational leader. He has no formal qualification in Design Led Innovation, but I feel he demonstrates the quality that all business leaders need to succeed into today's global economy. Peter has led the transformation of his company from a state of near bankruptcy to a world-leading designer and manufacturer of microphones. He has done this by not just focusing on the 'offering,' which are wonderfully designed products, but by looking at every part of his business from a customer focused perspective. I've had the pleasure of knowing Peter for the past few years and seeing his company grow from strength to strength, but the story I want to share with you starts well before I met him.

The company began its life in the 1960s as a sound equipment retail and installation company, which developed products for the booming local 'club' scene. Their early work had morphed into the booming disco years of the 1970s, where the company was growing from strength to strength, led by Peter's father. During the early '90s, when Peter had taken over the business, he was faced with a very different situation. The nightclubs were struggling and Peter admits that although he knew the audio side of the business inside out and back to front, his lack of business acumen exacerbated a crisis that saw him losing the family home and being a million dollars in debt.

Peter says the focus of the business has changed completely since those dark days, but admitted to me that in the beginning there was no plan. The catalyst was a cheap recording microphone he had picked up in China years earlier. Peter had the idea of improving it and selling it under his own brand. Touting the mic around shops and dealers in Australia, he was surprised to discover there was quite a lot of interest. The home recording market was on the rise, and slowly sales of the revamped microphone picked up. Essentially he stumbled into his own deep customer insight from which his business could grow.

Relying only on his intuition and fascination for the business, Peter learnt about his market from the ground up through reading, visiting factories and all kinds of trade shows. He was consciously making the shift from on the offering to looking at the customer experience as described in the *Doblin Ten Types of Innovation*. Talking directly with his customers led to a deep understanding and empathy with them. He had learned early on in his father's shop that most customers have a fear around buying technical products – they don't know how to use the equipment and often buy the wrong product. Peter solved customers' problems by simplifying products, making them more intuitive and showing his customers how to use them. This insight was embedded in company strategy. They couldn't just be a manufacturing company, they had to be a solution based business.

Although Peter hasn't undertaken any formal Design Led Innovation training, he exemplifies what it takes to lead by design and he's continued to lead this company with these principles.

To improve the quality, speed and profitability of new product developments while minimising the risk of failure, Peter sticks to timelines and performance targets at all stages of the development cycle. A policy of "constant incremental improvement" characterises *RØDE* 's value proposition for its customer. Innovating in the prototype stages, *RØDE* may send out a mic or software to influential people around the world as the product gets closer to market. They are offered a cash reward when they find a bug or flaw and *RØDE* gets to collect data directly from the customer. An added bonus is that when the customer is happy with the end product, word quickly spreads through social media.

It's in the approach to marketing where *RØDE* has been most progressive. Whereas they used to do trade shows and print advertising, they now exist mostly online with full-time employees working on social media and coding, as well as videographers and strategists. This dynamic website, which aims to educate as much as to sell, includes slick videos, fronted by Hollywood and music industry professionals, showcasing the how, why and wherefore of *RØDE* products under the label *"RØDE university."* Another successful initiative is an international short film competition launched in 2014, attracting entries from 76 countries. One of the films had 1.6 million views online and had *MyRØDEReel* written on it. *RØDE's* strategic investment into advertising and social media has given them tremendous reach into their market, ensuring they stay continuously connected to their customers.

Peter believes that the structure and culture of the company helps to add value to what they do. The company has a flat structure and everyone from the tech guys, to the marketers, to the industrial designers has a say in a product from day one. Peter sees himself as "Dad" - a strong personality, straight-talking, coupled with caring and empathy for his "family". He learnt that being able to delegate is also vital. The business needs to be able to succeed without him.

Peter is rightly proud of his contribution. *RØDE* has helped in democratising the professional audio industry and plays a role in education.

There is so much to learn from the *RØDE* case study - every time I speak with Peter I discover something new. The key point I want to illustrate is that the firm is not stuck on who owns innovation. It happens at multiple levels and there are multiple dimensions of engagement. Peter is a strong leader who keeps the company focused, but ultimately it is the firm's close connection to the customer which keeps them competitive and successful. As each staff member has a clear understanding of the company's purpose, the multiple types of innovation can occur without too much fuss. Staff are encouraged to experiment and take risks, but these are managed by staying close to the customer.

From an outside perspective, it could easily be assumed that *RØDE* are a product - focused company, which applies design only at Stages Two and Three from the *Danish Design Ladder* or at the 'offering' level as described in the *Doblin Ten Types of Innovation*. This case study reveals that *RØDE's* success lies in its ability to cut across all the different types of innovation and applications of design. The shift in thinking started when Peter received a jolt about his business; and it was his connection with his customer and understanding their needs, that enabled him to transform the company into the success it is today.

The four case studies used within this chapter highlight the need to shift how 'design' is understood within a firm. In each case, getting the firm to reframe and repurpose their understanding of design was a key part of the journey to becoming design led. This is never a simple task and it requires the support of a strong leader to drive this change in thinking.

In all the firms I've worked with, I've never seen an instance where this conversation has started with the design department. Including them early on in the discussion is critical. Design alone can't transform a company, but the process of design can assist tremendously. CEOs need to understand that design is a process and management capability. Designers constantly reframe problems, drawing out the contradictions and constraints, and they recognise there will be multiple answers.

The stories I've shared in this chapter demonstrate how company leaders can lead this change. The starting point isn't to defer to the design or marketing department, but to ask the question - is the organisation still competitive? The stumbling block isn't creativity or a lack of ideas, but having the courage to explore and experiment without necessarily jumping to a solution. This may sound inefficient, as the intuitive response will be to develop solutions and get quick wins. But if the solution isn't providing value to anyone, is this really innovation?

?

It's at this point that I'd ask a CEO … How is design perceived in your company and is this definition or understanding holding you back from exploring new applications within the business? Could the use of the *Cox Definition* of design, the *Danish Design Ladder* or the *Doblin Ten Types of Innovation* help shift this understanding?

The courage to transform an organisation is largely embedded in the mindset, which leaders need to develop, adopt and then spread out to all layers of an organisation. If there is a perception that design can only be applied to solve known product or technical challenges, the transition will be difficult to make. Adopting a design mindset across the organisation is core to the Design Led Innovation process. This will be explored in more detail in the following chapter.

notes...

....

....

....

....

....

....

....

....

....

....

....

....

....

....

notes...

i don't think this way, therefore my staff don't think this way

Are We There Yet?

i don't think this way, therefore my staff don't think this way

The phrase attributed to Peter Drucker, that *"culture eats strategy for breakfast,"* gets to the heart of this chapter. The phrase highlights that an organisation's strategy is only as good as the culture of its organisation. From my experience, an organisation's mindset is a key part of that culture.

The previous two chapters provided some insight into the journeys taken by firms to lead by design. Recapping, this requires strong leadership by the CEO to take a step back and look at their business and innovation practices from a new perspective, specifically with a focus on who is their customer; it also requires firms to question how they currently understand and use design and be open to new meanings of what value design can bring to a firm and how it can complement other innovation approaches across all parts of the business. As I shared some of the stories from firms who have begun their journey, a key component that was implicit in each case was the shift in mindset the organisation adopted throughout the process.

Leading by design starts with looking at business from the customer's perspective. This reveals new insights and opportunities to create a platform for change for the business. However, the bigger challenge comes in acting on these opportunities as this will usually require significant change within the business. Having the right mindset to undertake both of these tasks is at the core of the Design Led Innovation process and what I've learnt from engaging with firms is that shifting mindsets is not something that can be learned from theory; it must be experienced first hand and continually practiced.

Most of my interactions with firms are through workshops, which entail getting staff to experience what it is like to lead by design, or in other words to get them thinking like a designer. At the conclusion of a session, I normally ask them reflect on the programme and to write down how they would describe it to a colleague. The responses are quite similar and describe the need to shift from product to business model, spend more time on customer centricity and to get greater alignment of the customer to their entire organisation. The fact that firms are able to understand the concept of DLI in a short period of time is very encouraging but not surprising, as it makes good business sense to most.

However, I also ask firms what they perceive as the main obstacle of them implementing design led practices inside their firm. When I first asked this question, many years ago, I expected the main issue would be budget or the lack of funds. What I've heard, time and time again, is that the biggest challenge is that the organisation – particularly the senior leadership team - doesn't think this way. The mindset they experience during the workshop is at odds with the practices that currently operate within their firm.

Having the opportunity to follow up with many firms on a one to one basis, I re-ask this question and what has become clear is that the firm's culture doesn't allow staff to explore new directions unless they have a solid business case to justify expenditure; nor does it usually allow them to work with uncertainty and ambiguity around customer insights, unless they have rigorous market data, or better still, a potential customer ready to invest in its development. Getting it right the first time seems to be the only model, with no tolerance for exploration or failure.

A question that often arises is, 'how leading by design different to other strategy methods.' Sure, Design Led Innovation overlaps with many tools and methods that are commonly found in the strategy and business management arena. However, it's the mindset used to apply these tools, which mirrors how a designer is taught and works, which separates this approach to other standard business planning and strategy programmes.

Much has been written on the role of design thinking in helping businesses create new insights and visions for what they could become. Design thinking is essentially the cognitive processes that designers adopt to create new concepts, scenarios, products and services. They develop this approach to problem solving through their university education, which requires them to learn through practice in studio settings, as opposed to the typical lecture style format.

This is not the only thing a design education provides, as a competent designer will also have a depth of expertise in a particular context such as architecture, graphics or manufacturing, which they developed over the course of their education. However, it's their thinking styles that generally separate them from other students and professionals. More recently other disciplines have began to teach design thinking inside university education programmes, in particular business schools, to help their students deal with a level of complexity they will face in an uncertain world. I am of the firm belief that you can teach anyone the principle of design thinking and through practice they can master this approach.

However, where this often tumbles is the mindset of the leaders in the business. As I explained in Chapters 1 and 2, it's the CEO who needs to start the change and take responsibility for driving change within the organisation. I often see many leaders lack courage or time and outsource innovation to external consultants or to a department. The result is often a great idea, wrapped in a poor business model.

To overcome this, I suggest that the business leaders need to have ownership in the idea generation activity. By getting to know their customers and experiencing insights directly, they are in the position to best understand how their business can leverage the opportunity through new business models and changes in their current operations.

To achieve this, leaders will need to transform their mindset and stop thinking there is only one right answer. This opens the business to a process of exploration and ideation through design. This is called a design mindset and is critical to becoming design led. There's no point investing time, energy and money into applying the tools of DLI, without adopting a design thinking mindset.

To illustrate this point, I'd like to share the story of *Airocle*[1] and their CEO, Stephen Bird. Stephen was invited to participate in a government-run design programme and I spoke with him with mid way through he programme. As Stephen noted, before starting the programme, *Airocle* looked like a successful business – the largest designer, supplier and installer of diversified natural ventilation systems in Australia. Stephen told me their initial reaction to the invitation was why; why do we need this programme and advice?

It wasn't a coincidence. It was a case of perfect timing. *Airocle's* two main rivals had recently imploded and the whole market for building ventilation products had lost focus. The same old products were being enhanced, but there was a growing awareness and appetite for green solutions to ventilation problems, as well as the ever-present desire to keep costs down. "Customers and people in our channel to market - the architects, engineers and builders - were coming to us looking for direction on how to go about natural ventilation," Stephen told me. "And here we were, not really knowing how to respond, what new products we should be focusing on or what message to deliver and how to do that effectively." Sure *Airocle* was innovating, but they needed a new mindset to both capture insights from the markets and to align their business to these new opportunities.

As part of the programme, *Airocle* was asked to analyse how they engaged with their customers. This revealed that the conversation *Airocle* was having as a company with its customers was one-sided. It was all about the company, rather than the customer. "We were talking about ourselves and it was all about us. What was completely missing was the customer and that's what it's all about. You can get preoccupied with what you think the market is looking for, rather than what the customer needs and how you can help them," is how Stephen recounts it. It was that understanding that kick-started Stephen's change in mindset. The turnaround started quite simply with *Airocle* talking with customers and the people in their channel to market, and listening to their needs. This was done with some outside assistance, but the key was that it was *Airocle* staff who were working directly with the market to explore new opportunities, rather than looking for an immediate sale.

Part of this new approach was *Airocle's* team sitting around a table with the people in their channel to market - architects, engineers and design gurus - and taking a deep dive into what their customers wanted, with an open-minded challenge to generate ideas. Improving on current product and going to market on price was something they hadn't done before. Within a few months of this new approach to customer engagement, the team had come up with a shortlist of eight new products for development, with a company strategy to execute them. Unique design and performance created a unique value proposition, backed up by patents, ensuring there was nothing else like these new products available.

The first of the products into production was revolutionary, a new wind-driven turbo vent - something they'd never tried before. The reaction from customers was overwhelmingly positive and provided Stephen and his team with the confidence that the design led track was the right path.

Stephen believes that communication was at the heart of these

"We were talking about ourselves and it was all about us. What was completely missing was the customer, and that's what it's all about. You can get preoccupied with what you think the market is looking for rather than what the customer needs and how you can help them."

- Stephen Bird, *CEO, Airocle*

changes. Once his mindset began to shift, he started to involve other senior management and provided them with the freedom to explore new ways of engaging with customers and experimenting with ideas. This proved extremely valuable and the company now has far more direction than it ever had. Making all staff feel valuable, whatever their contribution, is part of their new philosophy. There's a lot more engagement at all levels.

What's the outcome of *Airocle's* DLI journey so far? Growth has risen 25 per cent in a short time; and their mission has gone from being an imitator to an innovator. "We do have an audacious goal," Stephen says, "and that's to be the world's best design-led ventilation company. But more than that, we want to make a contribution by delivering exceptional comfort in places of work and community and to outperform, naturally."

Stephen's story exemplifies what is takes to start the journey of becoming design led. As with the other case studies I've shared, *Airocle's* starting point was not a new product, which is where they had always innovated previously. It was in the process of speaking direct to customers and taking these insights back into the business to explore new opportunities and directions. What I wanted to make clear through *Airocle's* story is that Stephen needed to adopt a new mindset for innovation, as the market didn't give him all the answers he required. There was a great amount of uncertainty in what was being said and as a leader he needed to ensure his staff had the rights skills and culture to work with this level of ambiguity.

The design mindset of building empathy with his customers, prototyping ideas and not jumping to solutions, ensured Stephen and his team explored business opportunities, rather than jumping to solutions.

Making a mindset shift is one of the greatest blockers I have witnessed to the successful adoption of Design Led Innovation. Many firms are great at encouraging staff to think creatively, but as I mentioned earlier coming up with ideas inside a firm is generally not the problem. Having the culture inside a firm to tolerate the exploration of ideas that may not be fully resolved is the critical part. A core part of the management and leadership process within the organisation, is allowing this to happen to form a large part of a firm's culture.

Investing in design thinking as a management capability is key to building the culture inside firms. This will be required to tackle tomorrow's problems without the baggage of today's mindset. I say to my students, the CEOs and designers I work with; the only thing that separates the future from today is you and the mindset you bring with it!

As I mentioned at the start of Chapter 2, design has a long history that has allowed it to develop processes and methods that are unique to the discipline. A core of this is the design thinking mindset, which has been studied extensively and proven that it can be transferred to non-design practitioners.

The theory which underpins this mindset first started to

emerge at the turn of the 19th century, as discussed by the philosopher, Charles Sanders Peirce[2]. Peirce quite radically challenged the commonly held theory of logic at that time. Peirce's approach focused on looking at how we could learn from what happens in practice, rather than describing how it should happen. A high level summary of Peirce's contribution was to argue that 'deduction' proves that something must be and exist, whereas 'induction' shows that by looking at the outcomes you can determine or induct why it had occurred. To counter these two views he coined the term 'abduction' to allow for instances where a desired outcome can be considered, but cannot be linked to an understanding of how or what is required for it to occur.

Peirce's theory is heavy, but is easily found when delving deeper; but essentially it's this hypothesising of what may be, the act of producing propositions or conjectures, that is central to designing; and therefore 'abduction' should be thought of as the theoretical logic of design and therefore Design Led Innovation.

Nigel Cross, a British academic, a design researcher and educator, and *Emeritus Professor of Design Studies* at *The Open University* in the UK, has written extensively on the theory of design thinking[3]. He has built upon the work of Peirce by observing extensively how designers work. One phrase I particularly like about his description of the design process is that "designers recognise that problems and solutions in design are quite closely interwoven and that 'the solution' is not

DEDUCTION

INDUCTION

ABDUCTION

always a straightforward answer to 'the problem'. This description of design aptly describes what I believe is core to the design process, which is the process of learning by doing or more commonly referred to as prototyping. This is more than 'trial and error,' as it's a conscious act of using solutions to understand the core issues of the problem at hand, rather than trying to fix a problem. In each of the stories I've shared so far, prototyping has been a key part of the firm's design led journey.

I see many businesses focus on getting the solution first, thinking that it must be the right solution when they get there. They argue they don't have the time or resources to question assumptions and as leaders they should know the answer. This is where I see most businesses come unstuck. Their mindset doesn't allow for experimentation or tolerate failure or question, 'are we working on the right problem?' Therefore, they can only innovate what they can see today. With the problems firms are facing due to the massive economic shifts, a new mindset is required to question the fundamentals of the business. I see CEOs struggle because they feel they need to know the answer before they start, or as Peirce would describe, they would need to deduct or induce the answer before it occurred. Design Led Innovation provides an alternative framework to allow them to suspend getting to a final solution, exploring the real issues at hand. This is not different to how designers approach complex problems every day, except now the problem is not a product, house or website design, but a complex system called a business.

Other academics have written extensively about how design can relate to business problems or how as a society we need to challenge some of assumptions of what constitutes a valid method of analysis. I've included some of these references for those who wish to explore these ideas further. The key point I'd like to make and is that I've seen many CEOs who regard design thinking as a mysterious art and others whose lack of understanding of design ability see them trying to reformulate design activities in inappropriate ways. However, unlike in conventional logic, a design solution can't be derived directly from the problem, but can only be matched to it.

CEOs shouldn't despair that they need to become designers to develop a design led approach, nor can they outsource design mindset to their design departments! The CEO should aim to embrace a design thinking mindset, actively encouraging and leading change across the organisation. It's only by coming part of a company's culture that Design Led Innovation can allow a CEO to transform their business.

Theory is all well and good, but what does this shift in mindset look like in practice? The following story is from a company I have the upmost respect for. I met them when I was running a government design led programme for SME manufacturers. Throughout this three month programme I came to know *MEA*[4] and Joe Hoogland and Sonja Van Wegen.

Challenging everything that is accepted about what a company does and what it stands for is a brave move. Attempting it when things are going well, there is space to breathe and a budget to match is another thing – attempting it when turnover is in decline is braver still.

MEA designs and manufactures environmental monitoring systems. It turns data into information that can be used to measure soil moisture, renewable energy efficacy and plant science – invaluable to farmers and others who rely on the land for a living. The company had developed a highly reputable intellectual property and technology base. Significant changes in government regulation meant that a large proportion of their existing business model was doomed and they needed to act immediately.

That was the single event that shook the company up and forced *MEA* to cast its eyes around for an alternative business model. Although they already had a strategy for growth in place, the collapse of the industry accelerated the need for change. The transformation from being an integrator of components made by other companies, to a manufacturer in their own right, required *MEA* to concentrate their minds on exactly who they were selling to and what problem were they actually solving.

Joe and Sonja's story is one of true courage to ensure their firm remained competitive and successful. Over a period of 18 months, MEA set out to reframe and understand their customer, using the Design Led Innovation approach.

In speaking with Joe, he identified early that the challenge was not a technical one, where they felt most comfortable. Rather, it was a mindset one, which was preventing them from understanding their customers and putting systems in place to ensure they could capitalise on these insights. They needed to adopt an abductive mindset, but they didn't know how or what they needed to get there – a daunting place for any business to be in, especially when they face a declining market.

The change in mindset that *MEA* adopted didn't happen overnight, nor was it obvious at first sight, but once they were shown the starting line of the design led journey they were able to track their own path.

MEA's whole of company approach to the change experience has been beneficial, but harder to achieve than they expected for a company that prides itself on a social, inclusive culture. Through the process, *MEA* has identified their own "change champions". Not everyone in the organisation is up for change. There are people that get it, people that sit back, watch and then people who love it and want to run with it. The champions are motivated by a desire for purpose and a passion to pursue it, rather than the leadership and authority associated with the position.

Each time I go back to meet with *MEA*, I'm impressed with the progress they have made. They follow the three key principles I've mentioned throughout this book.

Firstly, questioning their innovation efforts relevant to today's economic conditions was imperative. For MEA, it was clear that a shift in government regulation would have significant negative impact on their business; the way they innovated through the development of great components and technology would no longer be sufficient.

Secondly, this led them to ask, 'if we are no longer a manufacturer of components, who is our customer and what value do we need to provide to them?' Most importantly, as *MEA* is not a large business, where would they find the capital for these new investments? The answer was that it could only come from stopping activities, which they were doing today and were no longer relevant. Stopping these activities is difficult in a small firm and therefore they needed to empower all staff to allow them to see and explore the problem.

This was the third key activity. *MEA* adopted and diffused a new design led mindset into the organisation to allow their staff to question who they were providing value to and how they could change. This new mindset needed to come initially from Joe, but he knew it also needed to pervade the entire organisation and to allow them to make the difficult and uncertain decisions they were facing.

Are *MEA* there yet? No, but they're a long way on their journey and in a much stronger position than if they resisted the need for change and focused on business as usual.

To summarise, over the past three chapters, I've started to share the key elements of Design Led Innovation, why it's vitally important and how firms have started on their individual journeys to use this approach to remain competitive. Although each of the journeys I've shown may be different, certain patterns are emerging in what it takes to lead by design. The key stages are :

Customer Value – This is the starting point. Ensuring a business is able to question if its innovation efforts are relevant by allowing itself to be clear on understanding who their customer is and the problem they're solving for them. This isn't as simple as just asking customers what they want, but in developing new approaches to re-engage with customers and partners in a company's future.

Strategic Alignment – Ensuring that all business processes, systems and products are aligned with the customer's problem is the next step. This may mean stopping activities within the current business as opposed to adding activities, which do not align around a common customer defined purpose.

Management Mindset – To build new insights about the customer and then to create the strategy to match will require a new mindset. This mindset will seem counterintuitive, as it requires the process of innovation to be 'slowed down' to allow new ideas to be explored and iterated with the customer. This will seem uncomfortable at first, as the data is not grounded in evidence and the process will force more than one right answer to be revealed. As I've illustrated in the stories shared so far, companies that have persevered have been rewarded for their efforts.

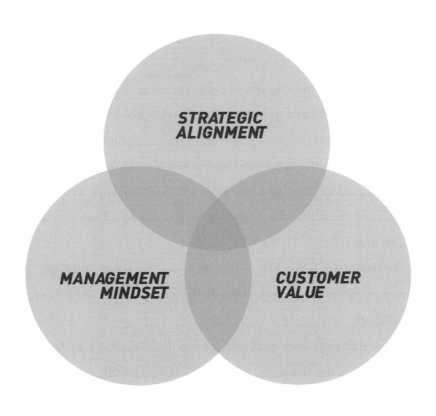

- Elements of Design Led Innovation

This is a good time to reflect on the mindset that a CEO brings to problems. How different is it to what I've described in the chapter? Answering this question may first require reflecting on how the CEO goes about solving the biggest challenges in their company. When was the last time something was learnt from a failure and why? When was the last time the CEO was surprised by something a customer said and acted on it?

Learning to think like a designer can be done, although it requires discipline to prevent falling back into old habits and jumping to a solution.

Now that I've covered off on what are the main stages of Design Led Innovation are, I'll focus on some of the practical steps to start this journey and describe some of the signposts along the way.

notes...

notes...

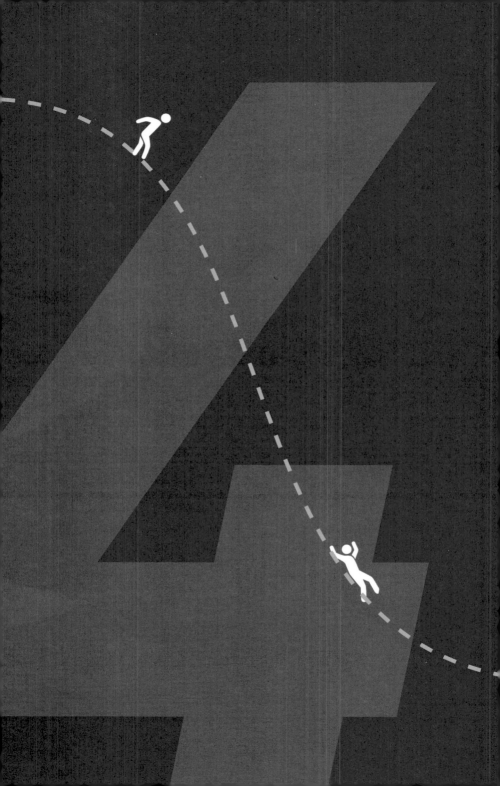

okay, you've got my interest...

where do i start?

Are We There Yet?

okay, you've got my interest... where do I start?

The bad news is that there is no step by step Design Led Innovation how to manual. The DLI approach is nuanced and the journey is different for every company. The good news, as discussed in the last few chapters, is that we can learn a great deal from the experience of CEOs who have embarked on successful DLI adventures and observe their journey, not to copy them; but to understand the lessons learnt along the way. I've explained the components of DLI and illustrated the way companies are putting them into practice in the first part of the book. Now I'd like to explore what the rest of the journey looks like.

It's vital to understand starting to lead by design can't be rushed. While introductory workshops have their place and can be incredibly useful to kick-start a mindset shift, developing the necessary capability and putting this into practice takes time. A CEO can't expect to introduce radical change and transform the culture of their organisation completely, overnight.   Nigel Spork, Managing Director of *Centor* took almost 15 months to develop a new business model. It's a huge investment. "Is it worth it?" is something I always ask firms along this journey and the response is always a resounding, "yes, absolutely!" What's important is that every CEO on the DLI journey had almost an awakening, followed by a long and unique journey. Although each journey is unique, I hope I've communicated the common factors and shared each CEO's own "eureka" moment.

"I'd like to say it was one light bulb moment, but
actually it developed over a 6 month period and then
the light bulbs just started going off. It started initially
as a light bulb every 3 weeks, then one a week
and then by the time we got through to 6 months of
thinking, it was a light bulb at the rate of 3 a day."

- Nigel Spork, *Managing Director, Centor*

As I've illustrated in the stories I've shared, change can be daunting. There are many best practices in change management, which can be used to guide this process. DLI doesn't aim to replace these, but works within these frameworks to support companies as they undertake their design led journey. I'd also like to stress that nearly 40 years of research by leadership and change expert, Dr John Kotter[1], has shown that more than 70% of all major transformation efforts fail. This is because organisations don't take a consistent, holistic approach to changing themselves and they don't engage their workforces effectively in the process. Therefore, a large part of leading by design is building staff development and capability in the process. This allows the firm to make the mindset shift as it grows. Change isn't a separate part of the process, but central to its adoption through staff development and empowerment.

Based on my work over the past 10 years of building up the theory of Design Led Innovation, I've started to see patterns of how leading by design can be undertaken. This doesn't detract from the uniqueness of each journey, but does start to give some signposts to help firms handle the transformation in manageable steps.

I've developed the following 2x2 matrix, which maps these key steps and signposts. As design aims to build both capability and strategy, in the same process I've mapped to the two axes of the matrix. I'd like to share some of the key steps, to provide insights into what lies ahead on the DLI journey.

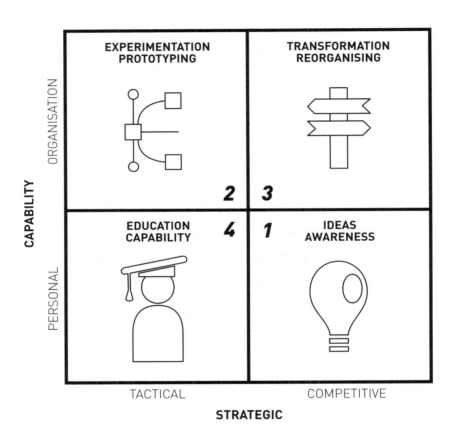

Design Led Innovation Matrix

What I've found is that when firms first experience design, they start from a backwards looking perspective and focus on getting staff skilled in design thinking. Therefore, I see these types of programmes sit in the bottom left quadrant – **Educational Capability**. They are normally called boot camps and they're usually very short in duration – often just a day or two. They're aimed at a broad cross section of staff from CEOs to middle managers and deal with tactical challenges such as how to engage differently with the customer, rapidly iterate ideas and generally becoming comfortable with high level design concepts and processes. They're best known for the amount of post-it notes that can be used in one day!

The benefit of the boot camp is that it teaches non-designers how to think like a designer. The trouble is, when staff go back to their offices after a boot camp, they require permission from the firm's leadership to start to apply this new approach to innovation, to experiment and iterate. As shown in the earlier chapters, this mindset shift is usually counterintuitive to how most businesses work and I often hear from staff who have undertaken such programmes that they feel caught between wanting to apply these new skills in their business and the business giving them permission to change the status quo of work.

Often what happens is that following participation in a boot camp, staff have had an awakening on a new way of thinking, but no outlet to apply it. Staff are left frustrated and employers questioning the value of sending staff on the programme.

Therefore, I prefer to start on the bottom right hand side, the Ideas Awareness stage of the matrix and then work on bringing the entire business along the journey.

For each stage of the matrix, I use a similar set of questions and tools, which allows me to have the same structured conversation with staff across the organisation. What changes is the focus of conversation matched to the level of seniority and responsibility within the organisation. It is the sequencing of these conversations, which is critical. Therefore, I forget the boot camp model as the starting point … what I believe is needed is to work intensely with all staff in the organisation to look at their whole business differently.

The format for each conversation follows what I have termed the 'Deep Dive framework', as it allows the firms to go deeper into understanding their customer. The key steps for the Deep Dive framework are outlined in the coming pages to give an understanding of the types of questions firms need to be able to address. However, remember these same questions are undertaken multiple times with different staff across the organisation to give a whole of business perspective.

deep dive framework

UNDERSTANDING
An assessment of the current business and its ways of innovating.

ENVISAGING
An exploration of new possibilities beyond the current business.

EMPATHISE
An understanding of the possible problems and emotions
of a future customer.

PROPOSITION
A new value proposition based on the assumed needs
of a future customer.

PROVOCATION
A description of the real meaning behind problems for customers.

RE-DESIGN
A new ideal but realistic value proposition and business model that
the company will consider.

CONNECTION
A new strategy to get towards desired state.

ALIGNMENT
An implementation of actual change.

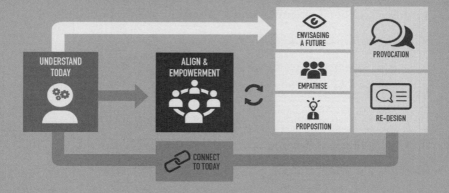

The starting point is getting the firm to **understand** the business today, so that any future mapping can be grounded in its current reality. The next phase is to get the firm to **envisage** an alternative future, completely centred around a clear set of customer needs, which can be developed by building **empathy** around a future customer. It is here that firms struggle, as they focus on reaching a solution, rather than giving themselves the freedom to create a **proposition** of a possible future solution, to fully understand what problem they are trying to solve – in other words, an abductive mindset. To validate and de-risk this future, I get the firm to speak with customers to **provoke** a conversation about what challenges the customers will face and the firm will need to address. Again I see firms trying to get into solution mode at this stage, rushing to provide solutions to the customer's problems, where at this stage they should be listening to the customer and then (re)designing what the firm believes a future value proposition will be. The next steps are to take the future state and **connect** this back to today's **understanding** to highlight where the gaps are and to pinpoint the opportunities. In doing so, the firm can begin to transition to the activities, which align the future with today.

This Deep Dive framework may sound straight forward, but as I mentioned earlier, the key is that it gets repeated across the organisation to allow the same conversation to build a shared understanding and highlight capability gaps within the firm. This model is also quite unique to SMEs, as their size allows this process to be undertaken across organisation in a short amount of time, with most firms being able to get to Stage 3 of the Design Led Innovation Matrix within three to six months.

If I now go back to the Matrix (shown on page 140), I want to show how the questions I just described can be applied to each stage.

The first conversation needs to be had with the CEO or owner of the organisation to get their buy in. Therefore, the starting point is at the bottom right side of the matrix – **ideas and awareness.** What I often find is that through this process the CEO comes to understand that their mindset is blocking strategic thinking within the firm. This is their awakening, their eureka moment, when they come to understand for the first time that "I don't think this way"; they usually work from fixing the problem, rather than envisaging a new future to understand the problem. A key takeaway is that they leave the sessions understanding that they aren't seeking a strategy, they're seeking something in themselves to change the organisation. This is very revealing and confronting, for them as leaders. It's this revelation that's the main purpose of the exercise. Once the CEO is on board, they want to know how they can get the rest of the organisation on board.

It's then that I get them to move to the top left of the matrix – **experimentation and prototyping,** where we start to, as John Kotter says, "build a collection of the willing, by building an end to end case study on how design can begin to add value to an organisation". However, we all know it's difficult to 'rebuild the aircraft while it's still flying', so what I've found works best is to take a set of leaders and key staff offline to work on a pilot project using the principles of design. The pilot, or 'deep dive' as I often refer to it, provides the context to build the capability and practical examples of what design could do.

With the CEO as sponsor, the team looks at the customer facing problem from a traditional point of view and then starts to dive deep from a new customer future perspective following the framework I just described. The selected team develops a new way of thinking as part of the process, while developing new ideas for the organisation. They project what the company could be from examining the business through this lens. However, they stop short by not unpacking all of the organisational strategy required to implement the solution they've identified, rather showing only a small instance of what could be. This stage can take up to three months. This is when it gets really interesting.

From this type of activity, a tuned in CEO and a motivated senior management team are now armed with an understanding of the approach and have developed some champions to drive the necessary change. The case study developed from the pilot can be used to start to socialise the idea within the business to describe the change required, gaps in the organisation and most importantly, the need to think differently. This is where the firm makes the decision to move to the top right hand side of the matrix - **transformation**

reorganisation and contemplate undertaking a complete transformation of the business by leading through design.

This isn't usually as straightforward as turning off the light one day on the old business model and coming in the next day and starting a new company that is now design led. Often firms start by going between the top left and right hand side of the matrix to undertake deep dives in various customer segments to build new awareness and thinking, before they are clear on what is actually required. This is where support from mentors, consultants and peers is critical, as the discipline required to be true to the process of design can be undermined when today's reality of time pressures and short term revenue targets creep into the process. (I discuss this further in chapter 6.)

Strategies on how this stage can be achieved could fill the pages of a completely new book, but my goal here is to introduce how the key steps on this journey may look. One aspect which is critical at this stage of the journey is the need to adopt a prototyping mindset.

Prototyping is a vital tool for designers, enabling them to learn about a product's flaws and improve and hone the product to better meet the needs of the end user. However, as I've discussed, you can also prototype a business model.

I've shared many examples of this so far … *Rinstrum, Gourmet Garden* and *Airocle*. Even though *Centor* already had a reputation for innovation and used prototyping for the design of their products and services, a new customer centric focus changed their approach to prototyping. Prior to developing design thinking, Nigel didn't look at prototyping as a way of solving a customer's problem or developing business models and strategy. Rather, he'd build a prototype as a final proof of concept. Now, he uses prototyping at every step. Nigel says the only failure he doesn't tolerate now is the failure to try something new and learn from this.

To reinforce how this approach can work in practice I want to share the following story, based on a project I ran with a wine region in Australia, to drive innovation in their supply chain.

Vince O'Brien is the General Manager Business Development at the *Australian Wine Research Institute²*, which aims to improve the profitability of the Australian grape and wine industry through world class research, practical solutions and collaboration. The Australian Wine sector is an extremely important export business sector and like many of the other fine wine regions of the world, has invested heavily in innovation to drive competitiveness. Vince was extremely experienced in the layers of technical innovation and how technical innovation can drive growth in the sector. He was particularly interested in exploring the 'softer side' of innovation, and had asked me to run a project with a specific region and their entire supply chain to do so.

Vince got to this point by initially working on an unrelated project, which allowed him to reframe the challenges in the wine sector. Without realising it and without being told, he had started his Design Led Innovation journey by building 'ideas and awareness' as per the bottom right hand side of the matrix. From this initial activity he understood that the design led process would enable him and the sector to build new capabilities, so as a collective they could innovate and drive change.

He therefore decided to start the next phase – moving to the top left hand side of the matrix (experimentation and prototyping), which was to bring together key industry leaders and wine makers from the *McLaren Vale* region to look at the sector from a new perspective. This was run as a series of four full day workshops held over a period of two months. He was not too sure what would come of this programme, but he felt it was a great place to start.

He remembers well the first eureka moment from the workshop – that as a regional sector, they were able to achieve radical changes, as opposed to incremental changes, which occurred within each business. The second eureka moment was when the group was using DLI tools to interview customers, who spent a lot of money on wine. He discovered they weren't just buying for the taste of the wine, but that they were chasing unique experiences. Not only did the wine have to taste great, it had to excite the customer's curiosity and feed their fascination for new facts.

This new insight led the group to believe that the biggest mindset shift they required was shifting to a consumer focus and that current innovation approaches were blocking this. DLI provided them with valuable tools for finding out how to build emotional appeal into the product – in his case, wine. This leads to customers becoming emotionally engaged with the product, and in turn, becoming real advocates for the product.

A smaller group was then formed to develop this insight into a business concept, where they could seek investment and prototype it with customers, which is Stage 3 in the matrix, **Transformation Reorganising**. The value proposition centered on the notion of a "Luxury Halo Brand" aimed at Baby Boomers, as it had the capacity to raise the brand image and profile of the *McLaren Vale* at a regional level, by associating it with a luxury experience. To provide some context, the *McLaren Vale* has a demonstrated capacity to produce grapes that go into some of Australia's iconic wines, producing some of Australia's best wines. Despite this, many wineries in the region trade in a crowded market, increasingly competing on price against low cost producers. Raising the profile and brand image of *McLaren Vale* would assist wineries in the region demand the premiums that the quality of their wines deserve in international markets.

The concept was refined by working with customers to develop a unique experience and business model to support it. The project is now titled *VALO³* and has been designed to have a "HALO effect" on wineries, winemakers and grape growers in the region.

VALO is a series of five unique wine events, each designed to generate a connection to the science, the art and the people behind *McLaren Vale* wines. Essentially, *VALO* is to wine as what *Heston Blumenthal* is to food.

Vince tells me that the project hasn't been without its

challenges, as they have essentially developed a completely new value proposition for the sector while managing to run their own individual businesses, which require them to revert to traditional approaches of innovation. Managing these two mindsets in parallel – today's business model and a future opportunity is what firms need to overcome constantly. This is the greatest risk in the process.

The *VALO* team is still on their journey and I look forward to following their progress as they approach the next stage. This will involve moving from the top right to the top bottom of the quadrant – **education and capabilities**. Initially the team will need to validate their new competitive strategy. Once they have built market acceptance around this proposition, they can begin the process of building capability in all of their staff around a common purpose. They couldn't have started at this point, as staff would not have had the permission to make the strategic business change. But now they've been given the go-ahead they can build sector level capability around a common purpose and continue to innovate with this new mindset and approach.

In summary, I've stood side by side with many companies as they embark on their DLI journeys. Completing the matrix takes time. In some cases, years. This isn't to say economic success doesn't come sooner, as firms will see value through the process, often immediately.

With sponsorship from the CEO, and the right capability, it can be done and it's proven successful time and time again. The thing with

DLI is that it doesn't stop – by its very nature, DLI implies constant reflection, revision and renewal. When a company reaches the bottom left quadrant, it's time to start the process again, and devise a whole new set of challenges. This is simply good governance and I encourage firms to develop this as part of their strategy planning process. They need to develop a culture of actively disrupting themselves to realise the missing link, before their competitors beat them to the finish.

When I speak with CEOs considering embarking on a Design Led Innovation journey, I urge them not to persist despite the work ahead. When I speak to CEOs who are in the midst of their journeys and are despairing that there's no light at the end of the tunnel, I can confidently assure them that the rewards are great in terms of company growth, engaged staff, and ultimately, very happy and satisfied customers.

Just get out there and listen (don't sell your company) to your market - it will help you understand how the market actually works and it will also help you decide who you want to choose as your customer.

- Glen Pacholke, *Centor*

?

I hope this chapter has provided an insight into the key milestone along the journey to becoming design led. Although each firm's situation will be unique, I've found that the four key steps in the quadrant are common to most. Here's a few useful reflections for CEOs and their firms.

How do they see this journey being played out across their organisation? What problem would they like to pilot a deep dive on? Who in their organisation could assist with this task?

At a more fundamental level a design champion recently told me of their approach; how they overcome the inertia of getting started?

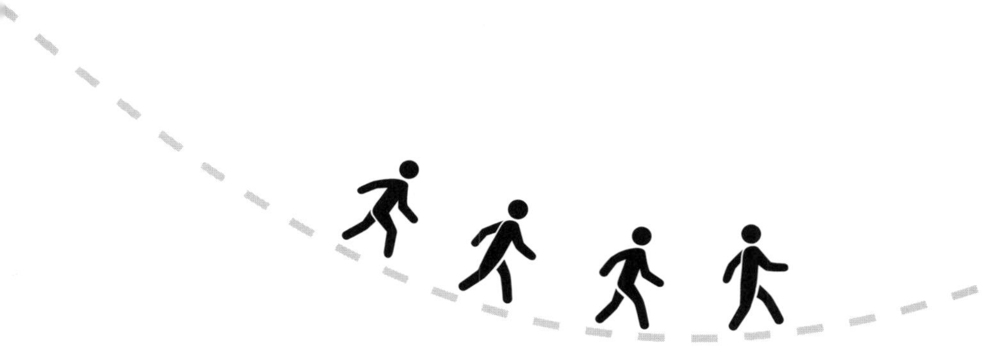

notes...

....

....

....

....

....

....

....

....

....

....

....

....

....

....

Are We There Yet?

notes...

....

....

....

....

....

....

....

....

....

....

....

....

what does success look like?

Are We There Yet?

what does success look like?

So far, I've discussed the elements of DLI, the long journey a CEO must commit to when they embark on transforming their business to lead by design and some of the pitfalls they will likely encounter along the way. It may seem hard, very hard, but the effort in making this shift does pay off. As shown through the stories I've presented, the results are reflected in a stronger economic position for the firm, but often and more importantly the creation of a workplace where all staff are aligned around a common purpose, which lifts the culture and productivity of the organisation.

Given this is often such a long journey, it's easy to get lost in navigating a pathway to success. So what does the destination look like and how do we know if we have arrived?

I hope I've communicated that leading by design isn't a destination, but a complete renewal of a firm's culture and mindset, which in turn changes how and what it innovates. Once you have developed a solid understanding of your future, it's a process of continual renewal to ensure your business stays relevant and resilient in dynamically changing markets and customer demands. So there's no end point … a company doesn't stop leading by design.

This answer is generally not what CEOs want to hear, particularity in the early stages of their journeys. Therefore, to help firms better understand what 'success' or 'good' looks like, I've developed a framework, which describes the key activities that describe what leading by design is. The framework is the result of my own work with firms, and studying successful design led companies. I had the opportunity to finetune the framework while working with a colleague, Peter King, on a report we were commissioned to write for the *Australian Federal Government*[1] to assist firms to better understand what is meant by leading by design.

The report was based on interviewing high performing, globally competitive, Australian manufacturing firms. These firms use design in its broadest sense to create and capture value. They were found to be purposeful and methodical in their application of design principles to all aspects of their organisation. They use up to date production techniques. Their highly skilled professionals and tradespeople work in modern surroundings and are led by innovative managers.

The key output of this report was the development of a Design Led Innovation framework, which articulates three key underpinnings of what it takes to lead by design: *Innovation Focus, Innovation Activities and Innovation Mindset*. The goal was to use this to help firms consider what the destination may look like and gauge where they are in terms of their journey.

Innovation Focus, the inner circle, is the major shift a firm needs to undertake – the shift from product focus to business model innovation focus (these points were brought up in chapter 1 and 2).

Innovation Mindset, the outer ring, describes the need to adopt a new approach to framing problems and understanding the customer within the business (this was raised in chapter 3). As previously discussed, realising a different approach to innovation is

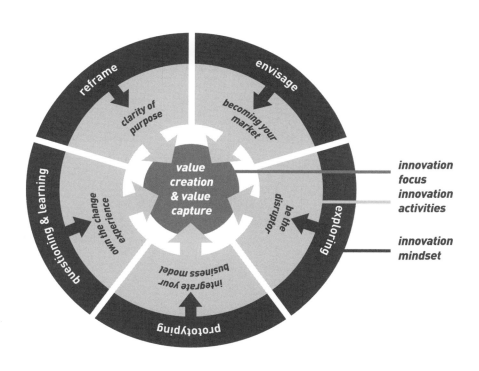

- Design Led Innovation Framework

163

needed and adopting a new mindset, is not enough; these must be applied to all activities within a business, which essentially means a redesign of the organisation.

Our studies show that it is the **Innovation Activities** organisations adopted, combined with the shift in mindset and focus, that is core to the success of these companies.

This chapter will expand on what these activities are and why they're important. As you will see these five core Innovation Activities aren't new or novel by themselves. When they're integrated in an overall business context, they enable companies to strategically maximise their opportunities to create and capture value. This, of course, leads to gaining a competitive edge.

I've drawn out quotes from this report to reinforce these key activities, which you'll see on the following pages.

I caution CEOs not to cherry-pick the principles. Alone, they won't work. They need to be used together, in varying degrees, depending on the organisation they're being applied to. This creates a dynamic and exciting environment that will prove challenging – but rewarding - not just in terms of a company's growth, but the engagement and satisfaction of its staff.

In my experience, companies on the DLI journey demonstrate excellence in each of the five key innovation activities, while being clear on their innovation focus and mindset.

"five key innovation activities

- ○ **CLARITY OF PURPOSE**
  know when to say no

- ○ **BECOME YOUR MARKET**
  organisation-wide immersion in the customer's world

- ○ **BE THE DISRUPTOR**
  change the ground rules

- ○ **INTEGRATE YOUR BUSINESS MODEL**
  design for integration

- ○ **OWN THE CHANGE EXPERIENCE**
  continuous renewal is the new status quo

clarity of purpose
know when to say no

Questioning the company's purpose is a critical first step for any efficient organisation. Clarity of purpose needs to be informed by a deep understanding of the market and guides all organisation planning and execution. Achieving clarity of purpose requires a reframing of business vision and values. It's long term oriented and sits at a high level in relation to business strategy.

Clarity of purpose is best achieved through a culture of questioning and open discussion of organisational purpose, vision and direction. It's essential that all staff are encouraged to challenge the organisational purpose, as part of an ongoing practice of validation and reframing. This whole of organisation approach introduces innovation to all business functions and levels of responsibility. An organisation that constantly refines and clarifies its purpose is better able to adapt to new developments, such as changing markets and the discovery of new customer needs.

Clarity of purpose also allows a company to critically judge its progress and prioritise projects and investment of resources. It gives the CEO the ability to understand what success looks like and to foster creativity and manage risk, while ensuring that the measurement of risk and uncertainty is well understood by all staff.

"You have to distil out what the company purpose is and build the company around it. Because we have great clarity of purpose everybody is working on the same thing....so this business becomes their (staff) business as much as it is my business

- Centor

"Our purpose is known through the entire team. I oversee everything but I don't have to micro-manage them, they know RØDE, they know where they are and what they're doing. Everybody can identify what RØDE is about and where we are going and they are all rowing in the same direction which is great.

- RØDE

"Our Vision Statement now sets a very clear direction for where we want to be as a business. To support this we went out to every team in the business and workshopped what our core values were. We've then been able to design a programme that everyone can be a part of and ultimately we aim to have everyone saying "yes" to the things that will drive us towards the vision.

- ENWARE

If a CEO wants to gauge how far along the scale of achieving clarity of purpose an organisation is, they can reflect on a few questions.

Can everyone in the organisation state its purpose? Does everyone understand the company's strategy?

If the answer to both questions is yes, a CEO should feel empowered in the knowledge that they and their team know what they do, why they do it and how everyone works as a unit to achieve success.

become your market

organisation-wide immersion in the customer's world

Immersion and deep empathy with the customer's world means engaging with customers as co-innovators, which makes sense as they are so heavily invested in the outcomes. The design approach to customer immersion imagines futures that customers can't imagine for themselves. I'm not just talking about traditional market research. CEOs need to delve deeper and listen to their customers and stakeholders, to discover latent needs and opportunities. This applies to all businesses, whether B2B or B2C.

Immersion in the world of the customer is a process of deepening empathy and has significant implications for organisational alignment. Immersion means that responsibility for understanding the customer no longer rests solely with the marketing department, but becomes company wide embedded in the culture and formally supported. Immersion in the market is also vital for organisations to constantly test and build on their value proposition, but CEOs can't stop there. To stay relevant and ahead of the game, they need to look beyond the world of the customer and gain empathy with all their stakeholders in the global value chain.

The outcomes of this approach are significant. Organisations need to clarify their organisational purpose by identifying exactly who their customer is, what they value and why. Understanding the customer's motivations (the why) allows exploration of value-laden business offerings (the what), corresponding business models (the how) and strategic partnerships (the who). This rich relationship with customers and stakeholders builds competitive resilience, as it's much harder to replicate than technological gains. Key competitive insights will also lead to opportunities for market disruption.

Once you understand the customer's Why, you can then go back to the How and the What. If you start with the What it is a field of dreams approach and you are reacting to what the market wants rather than looking beyond it and identifying exactly what your customer needs.

- AIROCLE

> *Getting deeper customer insights allows you to innovate in new areas and opens up opportunities we would never have considered. On top of this constant prototyping is a key part of building a relationship with customers rather than selling to customers.*

- GOURMET GARDENS

> *I think at some stage you've got to break from the voice of the customer because at some stage the customers knowledge is bounded by what they are used to, to some extent.*

- SEBEL

> *We communicate externally - we are driving the market and teaching them. We are constantly going where it's going and learning how we can predict and telling the end user what we are doing. We are not waiting.*

- RØDE

How does a CEO know if they and their team, understand who their customer is? They need to ask if every single person in their organisation understands the needs and motivations of their customer. This is a great test and I encourage every CEO to strive for this. It's more than staff knowing what the firm's mission and vision statement is … it's understanding the context of why the strategy has been developed, which has to come from a deep understanding of the customer.

This often requires the organisation taking the time to know the problems that their supply chain and stakeholders face, not just the end user's problems; and that the company's strategy is framed around the problems that it needs to solve for all their customers. A CEO needs to think about when they and their staff last allowed themselves the time to listen to a customer … not just about today's problems, but their concerns for the future. It's not just asking and listening that's important, it's what the CEO does with that information that's vital.

be the disruptor
change the ground rules

Actively disrupting itself is often one of the hardest tasks I've witnessed a firm struggle with. However, it's a critical aspect of remaining successful and competitive. The scale and pace of the global market means that competitive advantage through technological innovation is increasingly hard won and short lived. To be globally competitive means providing not only new products, but entirely new business models. This is a psychological shift from prediction via a rear view mirror, towards looking beyond the current market and envisaging new values and opportunities. CEOs need to be brave enough to consider entirely new directions.

I've talked about awakenings, eureka moments … that pivotal

moment of realisation in which CEOs question the relevance of their business. This jolt is the moment when the opportunity to create radical new directions is born. Realising the worth of this catalyst, several firms I've worked with have chosen to deliberately trigger these reflections periodically, testing the validity of their business model by challenging the status quo.

This kind of productive scepticism needs to be supported by organisational leadership that's open-minded and tolerant of failure. The ability to persevere toward ambitious goals through uncertainty and discomfort fosters resilience. Business creativity by definition challenges present-day assumptions and brave CEOs need to accept failure and change as learning opportunities.

> *It's part of the work we have done so far to integrate what we think the future looks like so we can actually take that next step later when we are ready.*
>
> **- GOURMET GARDENS**

> *It's about measuring yourself against what the potential is, lifting your eyes above the horizon even if we fall short and only get half way there, we will be challenging ourselves to be more competitive.*
>
> **- BRANACH**

Demonstrate courage to commit and follow through no matter what the situation. Commit to the finding and achieving ambitious goals – you will learn more from breaking the system than with you driving conservatively within yourself.

- CODAN

A successful disruptor continually responds to the changing needs and priorities of their customer and adjusts strategy and purpose accordingly. They explore making the impossible possible, rather than holding on the status quo. Their innovation activities include intangible elements of their business model and exploring new markets and customers.

A CEO needs to ask if they explore making the impossible possible, rather than holding onto the status quo ... who is responsible for this and what action is taken with the insights gained from this exercise? And does the CEO encourage their staff to think about disrupting the organisation or this conversation perceived as negative?

integrate your business model
design for integration

Broadening the focus beyond the immediate situation (in this case innovating at the product to the business model level) is an integrative practice of design. Business models are informed from identified organisational purpose, insights gained from disrupting accepted business practice, and integration. The use of the design approach in experimenting and adapting its business model enables a business to become agile to prioritise investment and to uncover new opportunities.

A guiding principle of all the companies I've worked with is their focus on innovative business models integrated with innovative products as drivers of competitive success. They all feel that alignment around the company's purpose and the ability to innovate through influence or ownership within the global business value chain is vitally important. Interestingly, this is where the biggest gains around value capture can be achieved.

It's important to remember there's no one correct business model. The right model for a particular business is developed by trying, learning and doing. In the same way manufacturers prototype product designs and refine their design and manufacture, CEOs need to be prepared to transform any aspect of their business model through a process of iterative trials and reflective refinements. Adopting a design led mindset will be critical for this to occur.

Moving away from a product-based view of business, towards a more integrative outlook where innovations may come from any part of the business model, means that no business function operates in a vacuum. Investment in intangibles such as brand, customer engagement, leadership and staff development are crucial. This is all supported by good leadership, focused attention to detail in execution and the ability to veto activities if they are not creating value for the organisation.

> *You don't innovate without design...so we design the way we go into business...we design the way we engage in business. Like all things you modify your designs as you go along. So we try things, if it doesn't work, we tweak it, we'll develop it.*

> **- FUTURIS**

> *It's the idea of actually having plans and strategies, design of so many different areas as part of an overall strategy, rather than thinking that design is just something – a design of a product.*

> **- IVR GROUP**

> *I am seeing design in a much broader context, in a technology company where the physical design of a reliable widget is mission critical, but it is only a part of a much much bigger scope to be successful.*

> **- RME**

A good test of seeing how integrated a business model is, is to answer these questions. Do we know our business model delivers value for our customer? Does our business model demonstrate that we care deeply for our channel and supply chain? Is our business model more than manufacturing a product — does it focus on the activities and systems that enable us to solve the problem our customer is experiencing?

own the change experience
change the ground rules

The type of organisational learning I've been talking about can only be achieved through putting into practice (known as thinking by doing or prototyping within design). This results in an ingrained tailored approach and a set of organisational values to innovation that can't be easily transferred or copied. The process is ambiguous at first, but through an experiential learning model DLI becomes part of the DNA of the organisation.

SMEs or any firm, need to become habitually dynamic to remain globally competitive. Evolution and renewal of a company ensures its continuing relevance in the market. Of course, day-to-day operations can't stop while business models, products and processes are being redesigned, so any change should be piloted alongside and incorporated into business-as-usual. This approach is particularly important to the CEOs who tell me they're too busy surviving to invest additional effort and resources in trying new things. I understand that consciously departing from a hard-won 'sweet spot' for the sake of innovation – when there is never a guarantee of success – seems counter intuitive. The only way to master the art of organisational evolution is to persevere and over time develop the dynamic capabilities needed.

" I think that a culture of not just continuous improvement, but continuous learning is vital. There is a need to replan, undertake self-assessments, adjust strategy and generally change the way we do things on the factory floor. If you stop doing that you're going to stagnate and eventually lose your competition."

- ENWARE

" It's going to start with people and culture. So forget what it is that the products or technologies or the markets are that we serve, we have a culture in this organisation that is about people feeling comfortable to respectfully challenge each other every day, okay, and we make it safe for people to do that."

- CODAN

" What I like about the design integration approach to some extent is the journey and I think that we're going to have a much better chance of changing things over time because it's going to [progress] slowly, people, they're going to get it."

- ROSSI BOOTS

When reflecting on their leadership style, CEOs often find it helpful to reflect on the following statements and how they apply to their company.

- Everyone in our organisation is a leader of leaders – we inspire and influence each other, rather than manage by control and command.
- Innovation is not just an R&D activity; we involve everyone in the company to help solve our channel and customers problems.
- Transforming our business is a long-term strategy – we will be able to manage change, while at the same time keeping our current model running.

The five key innovation activities are the underpinnings of what success looks like when a firm leads by design. When presenting these activities to a firm, I am often asked where the design element is to these, as they reflect more on the business than on the process of design. This is a key stumbling block when firms are tyring to understand how Design Led Innovation is different to other business planning techniques. Adopting a design mindset is critical and I'll elaborate on this in the following section.

A few years ago, I was being interviewed by a journalist who was interested in understanding more about the growing interest in the role and value of design. She'd heard of the term Design Led Innovation and done her homework on the key aspects, which she'd read in the popular press. Great stories but possibly a passing management fad was the attitude I felt she had before meeting with me. In preparing for the interview I sent her some of my research and gave her names of CEOs who I'd worked with, so she could get a deeper insight into the key underpinning of design and how it could transform an organisation.

When we finally met and spoke we had a wonderful conversation on why we need design, some of the barriers to its adoption and what success looks like. However, she admitted after the interview that she was still left with a bit of disappointment that there was no wow factor; she was hoping to see the silver bullet that design provided. She felt that Design Led Innovation was no more than good business sense. The results that were being achieved were impressive, but it was hard for her to make the correlation back to how design was responsible.

I wasn't surprised by the comment, as this is something I heard quite often when working with a company as they began to consider adopting design led practices. Comments such as, "yes I understand it, but why is this called design led – where is the design component?"

My response is that I agree design is a lot about common sense, but its real value is the mindset shift I spoke about in the previous chapters. This can only be understood when a firm experiences the process and doesn't just see the outputs.

The best evidence on the value of design comes from experiencing the process firsthand. I recall a session I was running for a family owned SME, whose management wanted to know more about how DLI could assist their business. Like many firms who approach me to undertake these workshops, the business wasn't in distress. They were quite successful, but knew there may be issues over the horizon. As part of the workshop, the CEO demonstrated the same behaviours as other CEOs I've talked about earlier … that they knew their market and doing a customer deep dive would not reveal any new insights.

During the course of the workshop we undertook a customer deep dive and a co-design activity, which the CEO was required to participate in. The CEO indicated that he was sceptical of the outcomes, but was willing to give it a go. I asked the customer questions and the CEO watched to form his own observations. To help with the evidence process, I audio recorded the session. After the activity, I asked the CEO how he thought it went. He was positive, but said he'd

"Design needs to be experienced and only when a CEO or firms goes through the process, do they see the value and understand the mindset shift."

heard nothing new. A few days later I provided him with a transcript of the session and it wasn't long before he called to check if it was the same conversation he'd witnessed and was part of, as he hadn't heard – or registered – most of what the customer said. The reason for this was that he was using an inductive mindset and constantly looking for solutions to what he felt their problems were and knowing he could solve them, rather than taking the time to listen. He admitted that without going through the process, he would never have believed that he lacked this capability or indeed understood the true value of a design mindset.

The moral of this story is that design is experiential and it's only by engaging with it that its value can be appreciated and reveal the gaps in your own understanding and thinking.

Although adopting a mindset is the critical part of starting a design led journey, having some quantifiable evidence that design does add value is still useful and can help companies take the first step in becoming design led.

There are many reports that indicate the positive impacts of design to a business's bottom line. Many of these studies directly report on how design has assisted a firm; others are less direct and focus on principles to demonstrate economic impact. There is some solid data coming from Scandinavian countries the UK and the US, as to the value of design to business. In a nutshell, theses studies find that design can directly and significantly improve sales, profits, turnover and growth, and a corresponding competitive edge. What's not to love?

All of these studies point to a very positive story on the impact design can have on an organisation. However, the real impact and evidence is not just looking at the outputs. As leading by design is such a broad and cultural shift within an organisation, I often find merely looking at economic outputs can be misleading. As leading by design requires a significant mindset shift and cultural change within the organisation, often firms ignore that to achieve the economic outputs requires considerable investment in the soft side of innovation, people.

To assist with this, it's helpful to go back to the three-ring Design Led Innovation framework and use this as a guide to assess how far a firm is from 'looking like success'.

?

I hope this chapter has provided answers to some of the key questions that arise in companies when considering to embark on a design led journey. I hope I've made it clear too, that DLI isn't a quick fix – it takes time. Design is an experiential process and CEOs need to spend time looking at their business through this lens. There's no A-B-C checklist that will result in a behavioural shift across an organisation; nor is DLI a set of tools or proprietary knowledge. It's about taking existing tools and applying them in a new way to a company's entire business, which will result in new outcomes, from products to business models.

It's my hope that by reflecting on the questions I've posed and the stories I've shared, that CEOs will open up themselves and their companies, to the huge potential for transformation and growth that embarking on the DLI journey can offer. Doing this is challenging and the next chapter will examine the support that may be needed to help with the journey.

notes...

....

....

....

....

....

....

....

....

....

....

....

....

....

....

Are We There Yet?

notes...

every journey needs support

Are We There Yet?

every journey needs support

The chapters up until now have focused on what firms needs to lead by design. Now I'm going to shift the conversation to what I believe is needed to support firms along their journey. Getting this support network established is critical, as I hear time and time again that it's one of the largest barriers to embarking on the design led journey. When listening to their concerns, what I'm often struck by is that companies, SMEs specifically, aren't looking for substantial financial support from government programmes to build this design capability within their organisations. Rather, it's the soft infrastructure they seek and are unable to find.

I'm often told that firms felt isolated when they began their DLI journeys. We know through education theory that deep learning around complex concepts, which is where I'd place DLI, occurs best when you have a peer network to work within. Having access to this type of network is a key a part of the soft infrastructure, which will be required to support firms as they embark on their DLI journeys.

I've facilitated the formation of these types of networks and participated with groups of CEOs who meet regularly to discuss the challenges of what it takes to lead by design. These CEOs constantly say the value of these networks is critical to support their ongoing development. However, these networks only occur if we start to see the widespread adoption of companies working and thinking this way. So what support do firms need to get started?

The following discussion develops ideas that I have written about elsewhere[1] and the key insights from these writings are that firms need both internal and external support, which I have referred to as Design Catalysts and Design Mentors. The capabilities of these two roles are quite unique and not easily found.

To support a firm on their journey to becoming design led, a Design Mentor and Design Catalyst need to be fluent and expert with the material I have presented throughout this book. At present there is no course or degree (that I am aware of) that will provide you with these skills, though many universities are working on this. In the interim, I've found that these experts have had a broad educational and professional background, spanning design, strategy, management, organisational change and psychology - to name a few - and are open to working with firms in new ways.

As I've illustrated with case studies, when a firm embarks on leading by design, one of the starting points is having someone who will challenge the fundamental of their business. This role I have termed the Design Mentor and initially, this person would be someone from outside the organisation and in many cases I have acted in this role. However, I know from experience that this role and expertise is also required internally and will translate into an in-house full-time role, which I have termed the Design Catalyst.

The Design Mentor is the person I see as responsible for starting a firm on its design led journey. They are there in the first instance to start the difficult conversation with the firm to challenge the firm's assumptions on how they innovate and how relevant their business is in a dynamically changing economy. When I've acted in this role, I've often found myself in some very uncomfortable conversations with the CEO.

The Design Mentor needs to approach this conversation from a position of neutrality and not believe they have all the answers or solutions. This is very different to providing consulting advice, as there is no problem to solve as no problem has been presented. Rather, the mentor's role is to get the firm to believe there are fundamental changes with the way they innovate. Many CEOs are not prepared to have this conversation and it often requires more than one meeting.

A level of trust needs to develop between the mentor and CEO; as with any relationship this takes time. However, once this bond is built the relationship between the mentor and CEO becomes one of the strongest and most critical as the company progresses along its journey to being design led. This is not to say the conversations get any easier, as the role of the mentor is not to be part of the fabric of the organisation, but to constantly act as the provocateur to challenge the thinking within the organisation and ensure old habits do not creep back in. The key role a Design Mentor undertakes is being able to challenge a business by constantly referencing best practices in Design Led Innovation.

The job description of the Design Catalyst complements the Design Mentor and often is confused with that of an internal designer. From what I have witnessed, often someone with design expertise does not make a good Design Catalyst as the very thing that gets a designer excited about design — the joy of creating something tangible — won't exist. When compared to designing a new product, there is no immediate adrenaline rush to be found in conversations about strategy. The heart of this role is working with people on organisational structures and innovation processes.

The Design Catalyst works closely with the CEO as they journey to becoming design led. Their role is to focus on designing the internal systems of the firm, starting with getting staff ready for the conversation they are about to have. This is where the overlap with traditional design practices emerges. Just as a trained designer understands the value of formulating questions, prototyping, execution and detail in a product, the Design Catalyst applies these same principles to the organisation itself.

Their role is not to lead the design journey, as this is the responsibility of the CEO, but to ensure that the strategy is formulated through a design mindset and linked back to a clear customer value proposition and then executed with the same attention to detail, which requires many conversations with staff. This is by no means an easy task. I've worked with many Design Catalysts and have seen that this role can be the most rewarding, as it involves being a large part of the change process. It's also potentially the most frustrating, as the Design Catalyst gets to see first hand the fear most people have around change and the defence mechanisms they put into place. A good Design Catalyst will have:

- Observational skills, as they will need to see gaps in their organisation and their market which any new organisational structures must align to. They need to identify these gaps and start the conversations within the firm.

- Communication skills, as they need to be clear and consistent on articulating the need for change and what that change will entail, while ensuring staff feel empowered around these decisions.

- Collaborative skills, as change doesn't happen in isolation and ultimately each staff member in the organisation will need to come along the journey.

- Enabling skills, as the role is not about providing the solutions, but empowering others to see the opportunities.

- Breadth of knowledge, as the role needs to manage conversations up and down the organisation.

As with CEOs needing a support network, I have found that Design Catalysts also need a peer network to support their development and address their feelings of isolation. Their discussion is somewhat different to those of the CEO networks, as they need to focus on strategies to deal with questions which inevitably come up along the journey. Often the Catalysts are seen as the 'rock' in a firm's journey, as they are the ones who provide the stability and assurance to a CEO and the organisation, that the benefits arising from the radical changes they are about to make may not be immediately clear and that they must trust in the process the results become evident.

These will be emerging roles and hopefully as more firms start to lead by design, formal programmes addressing these new roles will emerge. Until then, adopting a design mindset and 'learn by doing' is the best advice I can provide. If someone believes they would make a good Design Mentor or Catalysts, I suggest they start by meeting with a firm who have started their journey to lead by design. Understanding how their capabilities would match the company's journey and identifiying gaps in their knowledge, is a critical first step. This book is a good start, but it is only an introduction. The earlier chapters provide ideas about starting the conversation with firms in questioning their innovation practices or asking them to define who their customer is and think what the response may be.

For those firms who are looking for support, my advice is to connect to a like-minded organisation and start the journey together, as this journey can become lonely. Without the support of others, the risk is to default to old habits or worse still, to stall half way through. The design led journey is not linear and often leads a company down some rabbit holes to learn valuable lessons. Leaders like to believe they have the right answers all the time and that that is what their staff are looking for. SMEs often don't have the resources or time to get it wrong. However, getting it wrong is a key part of the design journey, as that's where companies learn most, providing their mindsets are attuned to capturing these lessons. Having a support network to help stay on track is critical to a company's success.

As I mentioned, SMEs are the critical backbone of most economies and we need them to continue to grow. If we build Design Led Innovation into these firms, they will reap the rewards of their efforts, but so will the entire nation and all of its citizens.

notes...

....

....

....

....

....

....

....

....

....

....

....

....

....

....

Are We There Yet?

notes...

some final words before you start your journey

Are We There Yet?

some final words before you start your journey

The focus of this book has been to start a conversation about what and why it means to lead by design. By sharing stories of firms who have started this and together with my experiences, I hope I've provided inspiration for others to begin their own journeys.

The starting point for this book was that SMEs are the powerhouse of most economies. These businesses are often forgotten when it comes to ensuring they get the necessary support to undertake innovation that's vital to them remaining competitive in challenging economic conditions. Given their size and the resources and time they're able to invest, what I've witnessed is that innovation in these businesses is clearly visible, but needs to shift. The focus is often on incremental solutions, developing tweaks to their business models and ensuring they remain cashflow positive.

Incremental innovation is essential for these businesses to survive, but survival isn't enough. We need SMEs to thrive, to ensure our national economies remain competitive and that we can continue to grow the standard of living for all the world's citizens. This is not to detract responsibility and attention away from the efforts of large business. It will be an integrated effort. My focus, however, is SMEs.

The companies I've had the honour of working with and whose stories I've shared in this book, are to be commended for being leaders and displaying the positive changes that can be achieved through DLI. I know there are many more success stories out there and we need to capture them to inspire others to accept the challenge. We're only at the start of the journey of creating the critical mass required to ensure our economies remain strong by encouraging SMEs to flourish. Writing this book and sharing these inspiring stories is a small but critical contribution.

Leading by design isn't rocket science. Although, I've seen businesses put up too many blockers as to why they can't make the transition, resulting in them getting stuck in a business model that's no longer competitive or relevant. Hopefully, my conversation has broken down some of these barriers and provided inspiration for taking the first step.

?

Here are some final questions, and corresponding advice that I'd ask a CEO to think about before taking the plunge.

1. Are my own innovation efforts relevant to today's economic conditions? And does my entire business provide value to my customer? (The hardest part to answering this question is figuring out how to measure relevancy and value.) When was the last time I stopped to ask ... and listen?

2. Does it feel like all staff are working towards a common company goal and purpose? Or does it feel like the business is getting pulled from pillar to post with conflicting agendas, priorities and resource demands?

3. How is design perceived in my company and is this definition or understanding holding us back from exploring new applications within the business? (A design led journey cannot be outsourced or delegated to a department; it requires leadership at the highest part of the organisation to start the conversation and navigate the journey. Don't get hung up on the term design, but understand its value to the business.)

4. What is the mindset I bring to problems? (Answering this question may first require asking another - How do I go about solving the biggest challenges in my company?) When was the last time as a business we learnt from a failure and why? When was the last time I was surprised by something a customer said which I acted on?

5. How long do I feel my business has to complete this journey? (Leading by design doesn't occur overnight and each firm's journey is unique. There are some signposts along the way to help navigate, but there is no step-by-step guide to follow. Once the journey has begun it's difficult to turn back, so readiness and stamina are essential!)

6. What does success look like for my business? (Rather than seeing this as the endpoint, use this as a navigational aid to direct decision making. It's okay to change direction along the way, as long as there is a clear understanding throughout all the company of the reasons for the change of direction.)

7. To whom can I turn when questions arise along the way? Who do I trust to confide in when I don't have answers about the future direction of the company; or when I think I've made a mistake and need guidance to see the lessons I can learn from that mistake?

These are the critical questions I've learnt from my journey with helping firms lead by design. Are any of the firms there yet? Of course not, as leading by design is not a destination but a journey of transformation.

I hope this book has inspired many to take the first steps in their DLI journey. It's up to all of us to make sure the movement continues, if we value our unique society and our prosperous way of life.

Are We There Yet?

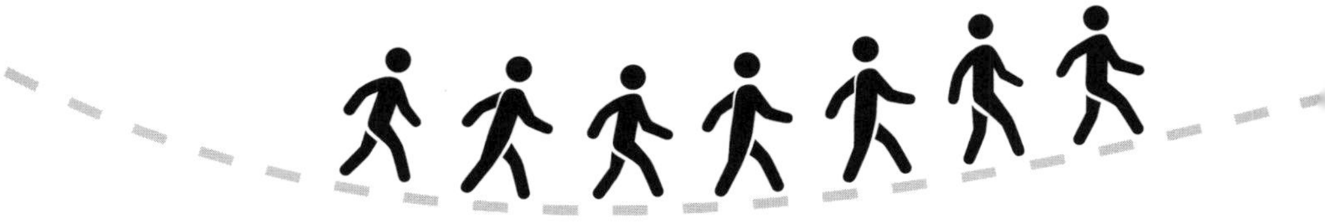

notes...

....

....

....

....

....

....

....

....

....

....

....

....

....

....

notes...

chapter notes...

Starting the conversation with Sam Bucolo

1. *Designing more competitive manufacturing firms* -
    http://minister.industry.gov.au/ministers/macfarlane/media-
    releases/designing-more-competitive-manufacturing-firms

2. *Design Thinking for Export Competitiveness Hub* -
    http://meta.org.au/hub/design-thinking-for-export-
    competitiveness/

Chapter 1

1. *Centor* - http://www.centor.com.au

Chapter 2

1. *Rinstrum* - http://www.rinstrum.com

2. *The Cox Review of Creativity in Business* -
    http://webarchive.nationalarchives.gov.uk/+/http:/www.hm-
    treasury.gov.uk/coxreview_index.htm

3. *The Design Ladder: Four Steps of Design Use* -
    http://ddc.dk/en/2015/05/the-design-ladder-four-steps-of-design-
    use/

4. *Gourmet Garden* - http://www.gourmetgarden.com

5. *Ten Types of Innovation: The Discipline of Building Breakthroughs* -
    https://www.doblin.com/tentypes/

6. *How BMW put innovation in the driver's seat* -
    http://www.uts.edu.au/about/uts-business-school/news/
    how-bmw-put-innovation-driver's-seat

7. *RØDE Microphones* - http://en.rode.com

Chapter 3

1. *Airocle* - http://www.airocle.com.au

2. *Charles Sanders Peirce* - http://www.peirce.org
   and http://plato.stanford.edu/entries/peirce/#dia

3. Nigel Cross Design Thinking: Understanding How
   Designers Think and Work - http://oro.open.ac.uk/39437/

4. MEA - http://mea.com.au

Chapter 4

1. *Kotter International* - http://www.kotterinternational.com

2. *Australian Wine and Research Institute* - http://www.awri.com.au

3. Valo - http://valowine.com

Chapter 5

1. *Designing more competitive manufacturing firms* -
   http://minister.industry.gov.au/ministers/macfarlane/media-
   releases/designing-more-competitive-manufacturing-firms

Chapter 6

1. *Design Mentors and Catalysts*

Andersen, Lisa, Paul Ashton and Lisa Colley (Eds). 2015. *Creative business in Australia: Learnings from the Creative Industries Innovation Centre*, 2009 to 2015. Broadway, NSW: UTS ePress. doi:10.5130/978-0-9924518-2-0

Bucolo, Sam and Wrigley, Cara (2014) Design Led Innovation : overcoming challenges to designing competitiveness to succeed in high cost environments. In Roos, Gooran and Kennedy, Narelle (Eds.) *Global Perspectives on Achieving Success in High and Low Cost Operating Environments.* IGI Global, pp. 241-251.

contacting sam...

Email
Sam.bucolo@uts.edu.au

Linked in
https://au.linkedin.com/pub/sam-bucolo/6/993/a8a

Dr Sam Bucolo is a Professor of Design Innovation at UTS, whose role is to help Australian business grow through Design Led Innovation, while ensuring university programmes evolve to match this structural industry shift. Sam was one of the original founders of the term Design Led Innovation, based on his work in getting firms to shift their focus from Technology Led Innovation models. Sam has collaborated widely with a range of industry partners; he has led many government initiatives on embedding Design Led Innovation within organisations; he has held several senior positions within Universities and was a former entrepreneur. He currently heads the Australian Design Integration Network and is the elected Australian board member for Cumulus, which represents over 200 art, design and media universities in 48 countries.

You can read about Sam's work at *The Design Innovation research centre* at *http://www.uts.edu.au/research-and-teaching/our-research/design-innovation-research-centre*.

Are We There Yet?